MW00329320

Northwest Ski Area Guide

Northwest
SKI AREA
GUIDE

for
Downhill &
Cross-country Skiers,
Snowboarders
& Snowplayers

Cookie
Crosetto

JOHNSTON
ASSOCIATES
INTERNATIONAL

P.O. BOX 313
MEDINA, WASHINGTON 98039
(206) 454-7333

Copyright © 1994 by Cookie Crosetto

All rights reserved. No part of this book may be reproduced or transmitted in any form or by any means, electonic or mechanical, including photocopying, recording or by any information storage and retrieval system, without written permission of the publisher.

The listings and information appearing in this edition were current at the time of final editing, but are subject to change at any time. No gratuities of any kind have been solicited or accepted from listed ski areas, accomodations, or businesses, etc. Ski area and state maps contained within are generalized illustrations. For specific information and directions, refer to a trail map provided by each ski area or an official state highway map.

Cover design and area illustrations by Mike Jaynes.
State maps by Marge Mueller.

Cover photos:
Alpine skiers, courtesy of Bogus Basin. Photo by Lew Peterson.
Snowboarder, courtesy of Jonas Roeser. Photo by Matt Woxland.
Mono-skier, Jonathon McKanna, courtesy of SKIFORALL. Photo by Corky Trewin.
Cross Country skiers, courtesy of Ski Lifts Inc. Photo by Kelly O'neil.

JASI Publications
PO Box 313
Medina, WA 98039

Library of Congress Cataloging-in-Publication Data

Crosetto, Cookie, 1943-
    Northwest ski area guide for downhill and cross country
skiers, snowboarders, and snowplayers /Cookie Crosetto
      p.   cm.
    ISBN 1-881409-09-0 $9.95
    1. Skis and skiing--West (U.S.)-- Guidebooks. 2. Skis and skiing
--West (U.S.)--Directories. 3. Mountains--West (U.S.)
--Recreational use --Directories. 4. West (U.S.)--Guidebooks.
    I. Title.
GV854.5.W 4C76 1994
796.93'0978--dc20   93-40421
                                                 CIP

Printed in the United States of America

DEDICATION

TO MY FATHER, WHO TAUGHT ME HOW TO SKI

TO MY BROTHERS, WHO CHALLENGED ME

TO MY SONS, WHO INTRODUCED ME TO RACING

TO MY HUSBAND, WHO KEEPS ME ON THE SLOPES

INTRODUCTION

I love to ski! I love to re-discover familiar areas and experience new ones. There are forty-nine ski areas in Washington, Oregon and Idaho. It is my hope that by using the information in this book and your own desire to experience a new mountain, you too will find many new fun places to ski and vacation.

However, please keep in mind that the information presented in this book is intended for you to *use as a guide.* I have made every effort to be accurate with the information. Nevertheless, as I researched the areas, I found that all are making yearly changes, from lift ticket prices to amenities. I am confident though, that once you start to travel and experience each of these unique ski areas, you will soon add your own information.

As we are all too aware, anytime you partake in outdoor activities (especially in the winter), you risk experiencing Mother Nature at her best or worst. Ski conditions can change so quickly that it would be unfair to judge any ski area by a one day, week, or weekend experience. Also, as my family is quick to remind me, that while I prefer groomed, smooth runs, there are others who like deep powder, moguls, tree skiing, "the steeps", cliffs, or packed powder conditions. Some skiers are never bothered by adverse weather conditions, while others won't leave the lodge (or home) unless the sun is shining.

Keep in mind as you plan your trips that there is great diversity (facilities, prices, snow, grooming, etc.) in all the ski areas listed. But whatever you like in the way of skiing, you are sure to find it in these Pacific Northwest areas.

One of the reasons that I enjoy skiing so much is the friendliness of the people who work and participate in this sport. My thanks to the many skiers who shared a chairlift ride, their favorite runs, their ski area history, and their "local" information with me. My thanks also to the many employees who took time to visit and answer my endless questions. This book would not be possible without their friendly assistance and camaraderie.

GO SKI IT!

Cookie

TABLE OF CONTENTS

GENERAL INFORMATION

ACCOMMODATIONS The motels, condos, inns, etc. listed are selected from brochures and advertisements, as well as my experiences. Prices vary along with the accommodations. To save money and be more assured of a selection of places to stay, consider traveling at non-peak times (peak times are: Christmas, President's weekend, spring vacations and weekends). I prefer to stay in places which have easy (and short) walking distances from car to room. There is nothing more exhausting than loading and unloading skis, boots, poles, clothes, and food from a parking lot that is a block away from your room. B and B's are another option, and several are listed in this guide. Be sure to inquire if ski packages are available or if there are special packages which offer *free* or discounted accommodations for children.

CHILD CARE Child care facilities vary with each ski area. I found most of the facilities well-designed and the personnel delightful. Without exception, the facilities at the resort ski areas were excellent. I would advise that you always call first to make reservations. Fees are usually based on an hourly rate or by the ages of the children.

Things to consider before you leave your child are: is the facility state licensed, how many children are using the facility, how many adults are supervising and their qualifications, what activities are available, are the facilities closed for lunch, do the activities include outside play or ski lessons? Remember that you are responsible for bringing diapers, bottles, extra clothing, personal belongings, and usually lunch. Be sure to have your child's items marked.

CLOTHING It is helpful to have a basic check-list to refer to before you leave on your trip. There is nothing that can ruin a trip faster than forgetting something at home. Skis, boots, socks, gloves, hat, goggles, coat and pants are your basic list. (I am assuming that you are wearing your long underwear!) Additional items to include are: rain gear, extra gloves, sun protection for lips and skin, sun glasses, an extra set of long underwear, plus a change of shirts or sweaters. You may not need everything you take, but it is a bonus to be prepared for weather changes. Remember to layer for warmth.

CREDIT CARD USE Most ski areas accept Visa or Mastercard to purchase lift tickets. Most areas require a credit card or cash deposit, and a driver's license to rent equipment.

DRIVING TIMES The times given for traveling are based on an average winter driving speed of 55 mph. Even though the interstate freeways are now 65 mph, most of winter driving is slower. Also, all of the roads from the interstates to the ski areas are two-lanes with speed limits at a maximum of 45 mph, so I have included this in the average times estimated for travel. Always drive with caution, turn on your headlights on the two-lane roads, and take your time. THINK SAFETY!

LIFT TICKET PRICES Most prices listed reflect the prices for the 1993-94 ski season, unless noted. (As we go to press, some areas were still making pricing decisions.) The general rule to apply in future years is that lift prices have yet to go down. For the budget-minded skier, there are reduced lift prices on weekdays at most of the ski areas (the lines are shorter too). Half-day and night skiing tickets are usually a lower rate as well. There are special ski weeks advertised as well as ski packages (room and lift ticket) offered by motels/hotels. As you arrive in a ski area, check local publications for coupons or special promotions from local businesses offering discounts on lift tickets. Many ski areas have special prices for senior skiers (age 62 or 65+), students, college students, children under six, military and their dependents, and skiers with disabilities. Some areas give discounts if you show them a current season's pass from another area. They **do require current ID** for these discounted tickets though, so come prepared. If you plan your trip well in advance to major resorts, there are sometimes non-refundable, pre-season lift tickets available at a reduced price.

OPERATIONS Generally, the ski areas listed operate from mid-November to mid-April. Remember that ski areas operate depending on the weather conditions. Times and days of operation can change from the regular schedule at the whim of Mother Nature. Call the area before you leave home.

PARK 'N SKI PERMITS (IDAHO) These permits finance much of the cross country skiing in Idaho and also provide a funding source for ski clubs and agencies who maintain and develop cross country facilities. An annual permit is $15, a three-day temporary permit is $7.50. Permits are available from the Idaho Department of Parks and Recreation, Statehouse Mall, Boise, ID 83720-8000. **(208) 327-7444.**

PHONE LISTINGS Information phone lines at each ski area are generally answered by a live person. Snowline phone numbers are usually a recording.

PLAN A SAFE TRIP When planning any trip in the winter, it is best to follow the Boy Scout motto, "Be Prepared." Be prepared with equipment for road emergencies and always drive with caution. Help, which can be an ambulance or tow truck, can be a long time coming when you are on a mountain pass. Take time to check your car's mechanical functions and make sure it is winterized. Our car always has first aid supplies, a shovel for digging out of parking lots and ditches, a window scraper, a small broom, chains, sleeping bags or blankets, a flashlight, flares, extra food and water, lock and window de-icer, road maps, toilet paper, chains, a tarp or scrap of rug to lie on while putting on chains, and a jumper cable. It is amazing what conditions you can tolerate when you are prepared. Even though you think you have everything, it is still a good idea to call ahead for road, weather, and ski area conditions before you leave home.

PROTECTING YOUR EQUIPMENT Unfortunately, theft does occur at ski areas. My recommendation is to mark your equipment with your name, use the ski or basket checks when taking a break, and keep your extra ski equipment **undercover** in your car. Better a long walk back to the car for your extra gear than an expensive trip to the store to replace stolen articles.

RENTALS All areas renting alpine equipment include boots, poles and skis. Snowboard rentals include the board and boots. Cross country rentals include boots, poles and skis. Don't be tempted to "fudge" about your skiing ability or weight when renting equipment. Your safety depends on being fitted with proper equipment for your skill level. Also important are your

weight, height, sex, and age, which help determine the
binding tension, and the length, style and stiffness of the ski.
(You will need ID and usually a credit card and/or cash deposit
to rent equipment.)

RESERVATIONS I highly recommend calling ahead for
overnight accommodations at any ski area or nearby town.
(Even when there seems to be a large selection of motels, etc.)
When you call, be sure to inquire about ski packages. In some
cases special rates, lift tickets, continental breakfasts, or
children ski and stay *free*, will be included in your room price.
A great way to save $$$$$'s.

SKI SCHOOLS/SKIER DEVELOPMENT Most of the ski
areas listed have resident PSIA (Professional Ski Instructors of
America) ski schools operating. The schools offer all levels of
ski lessons on an hourly, half-day or full-day schedule. Areas
which offer snowboarding and cross country rentals usually
have instructors and classes available as well. I do advise that
you call to make reservations (most areas require it), especially
if you have young children or a group you wish to place in a
lesson. Many areas offer beginning or introductory ski packages
which include rental equipment and lessons. Quite a few areas
have staff capable of teaching persons with disabilities as
well as other special programs available. Call to inquire about
the type of program you may require.

SKIWEE This is a ski instruction program for children ages
four to twelve, usually by reservation only and includes a lift
ticket, lesson and lunch, with or without rentals. It is offered at
most of the Oregon ski areas.

SNOWBOARDING Snowboarding is now generally accepted
at all ski areas listed. Areas which have special snowboarding
areas and/or facilities such as half-pipes are noted under the
Snowboarding category for each area.

SNOWPARKING PERMITS (OREGON) Permits to park in ski
area parking lots and designated off-highway locations are
required in Oregon winter recreation areas from November 15 to
April 30. These locations are adjacent to cross country ski trail
access points and major snowmobile sites, as well as within ski

areas. The only exception to this requirement is the Mount Bachelor ski area. Parking in designated areas without permits may result in a fine. Permits are sold at all ski areas, many sporting goods stores, and motor vehicle division offices throughout the state. You can purchase a season permit for $9.50, or pay a daily parking fee, which varies from $1.50 to $2. Current Washington, California, and Idaho permits are honored in Oregon. Remember to display them in your car window.

SNOWPARKING PERMITS (WASHINGTON) The sno-park permit includes over 70 locations which offer access to snowmobiling and cross country skiing areas. To purchase a Sno-park permit, send $20 to the Office of Winter Recreation, Washington State Parks and Recreation Commission, 7150 Cleanwater Lane KY-11, Olympia, WA 98504. Permits can also be purchased from County Auditors and retail locations. Washington permits are honored in Oregon and Idaho.

SUMMER OPERATIONS Some areas have extended operations. Late spring and early summer skiing is available at the Mount Bachelor and Timberline ski areas in Oregon.

TRAVELING WITH A LARGE GROUP Many ski areas have special group rates and party and banquet facilities available. Be sure to inquire.

TRAVELING BY BUS, TRAIN, OR PLANE If you don't like winter driving, many areas are already "destinations" on regularly scheduled public transportation routes. Check with a travel agent or call the transportation reservationist of your choice. Mention your destination and ask about any special or travel packages for that area. You'll be pleasantly surprised!

SKIERS' RESPONSIBILITY CODE

PLEASE KEEP IN MIND THAT THERE IS A SERIOUS AND RESPONSIBLE SIDE TO ALL WINTER SPORTS. EVERYONE (ESPECIALLY CHILDREN) SHOULD BE MADE AWARE OF THIS PART OF THE SPORT.

You will see the following list on many area brochures and trail maps. These are excellent guidelines, but are only a partial list.

1. Ski under control and in such a manner that you can stop or avoid other skiers or objects.

2. When skiing downhill or overtaking another skier, you must avoid the skier below you.

3. You must not stop where you obstruct a trail or are not visible from above.

4. When entering a trail or starting downhill, yield to other skiers.

5. All skiers must wear retention straps or other devices to help prevent runaway skis.

6. Keep off CLOSED trails and posted areas and observe all posted signs--especially those designated as slow skiing areas.

In addition to the skier's responsibility code, there are other legalities of which skiers should be aware. One law is: "state law provides that any person skiing outside the confines of designated trails or runs open for skiing within the ski area boundary shall be responsible for any injuries or losses resulting from his or her action."

The ski area drawings provided in this book are to give you a pictorial overview of the ski area and are **not to be used as a trail map**.

Designated trails and runs are identified on a trail map provided by each ski area. Before you ski any area new to you, be sure to obtain a trail map and **study it**! Ask questions of ski patrol and/or ski area personnel if the area is unfamiliar to you.

Know your own ski abilities and ski safely. Never allow others to make decisions for you. Know the ski area before you get on the hill. Also, each ski area has a boundary. Skiing beyond a boundary is risking your life. There are avalanche areas, unmarked obstacles and other hazards which exist in each ski area. Enjoy the designated ski area only. Be a responsible skier.

TRAIL MARKINGS

The symbols shown here comprise the standard International Trail Marking system. These symbols are *not absolute*. They describe only the relative degree of challenge of a particular trail when compared with all other trails *at that ski area*. Which means that a black diamond will not be the same degree of difficulty at all areas.

GREEN CIRCLE
Easier Trails and Runs
(Beginner)

BLUE SQUARE
More Difficult Trails and Runs
(Intermediate)

BLACK DIAMOND
Most Difficult Trails and Runs
(Advanced)

**DOUBLE
BLACK DIAMOND**
Caution, Expert Trails and Runs

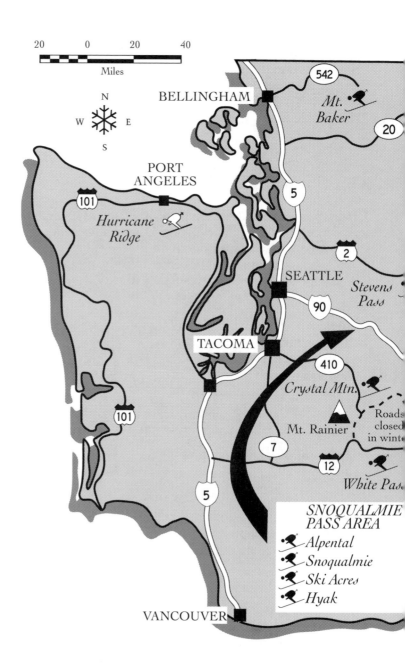

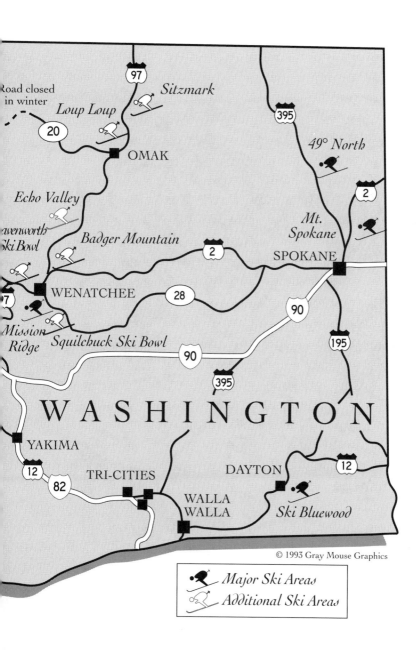

Road closed in winter

Loup Loup

Sitzmark

97

395

49° North

20

OMAK

Echo Valley

avenworth
Ski Bowl

Badger Mountain

Mt.
Spokane

2

SPOKANE

7

WENATCHEE

28

90

Mission
Ridge

Squilchuck Ski Bowl

90

195

395

W A S H I N G T O N

YAKIMA

DAYTON

12

12

TRI-CITIES

82

WALLA
WALLA

Ski Bluewood

© 1993 Gray Mouse Graphics

Major Ski Areas
Additional Ski Areas

ALPENTAL AREA

5,400' top elevation   **2,200' vertical drop**

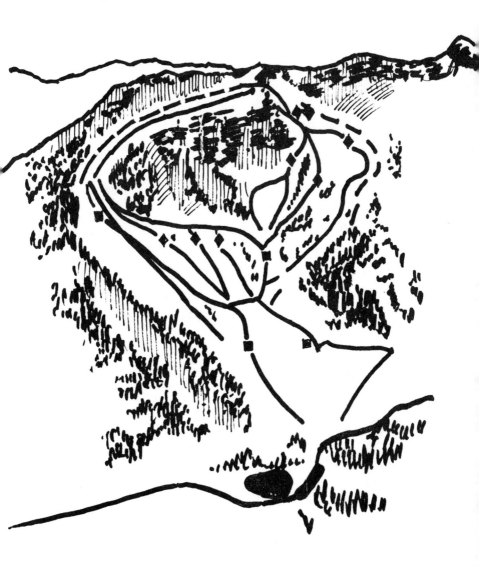

ALPENTAL

Alpental is the highest of the four ski areas at the summit of Snoqualmie Pass, rising above the others by 1,500 feet. From the parking lot, skiers cross a creek on a covered bridge and walk under a sky-bridge to reach the base of the ski area and the lodges. The mountain that rises dramatically before you supports the belief that this ski area is most attractive to advanced skiers. The experts love to brag about the sensational back-country skiing and the upper black diamond runs like "International" and "Adrenalin." However, there is a gentle beginner hill and some interesting intermediate runs on the lower slopes, so those groups or families with varied abilities can find happiness skiing together here.

The two-part Denny Mountain Lodge combines old and new in design, and both areas are uniquely connected by a sky bridge. You will find the "area regulars" gathered in the "old side," where the worn wooden chairs, floors and tables speak of years of noontime breaks and warming cold hands before the fire. The newer side is a modern design and provides a view of the lower slopes for observers. The menu caters towards healthy entrée choices, but for many, the favored lunch special is a "grinder."

The "Debbie's Gold" run on the mountain honors Debbie Armstrong, Olympic Gold Medalist in Giant Slalom in 1984. Debbie learned to ski at Alpental and started her racing career as a member of the Alpental Racing team, competing in Pacific Northwest Ski Association races. She continues to be a national and international figure in ski racing.

PHONE NUMBERS:

Snowline	(206) 236-1600
Information	(206) 434-SNOW
Lodge	(206) 434-6112
Ski School	(206) 434-6364
Road Conditions	(206) 455-7900
	1-900-940-PASS (35¢)

DIRECTIONS:
Alpental is located east of Seattle on I-90 at the summit of Snoqualmie Pass. It is 1.2 miles from the Snoqualmie Summit Ski Area on the Alpental Road. Exit 52 or 53.

DRIVING TIMES: (estimated)

Seattle	43 miles	45 minutes
North Bend	21 miles	30 minutes
Cle Elum	30 miles	30 minutes
Spokane	257 miles	4.5 hours
Portland	227 miles	4 hours
Boise	448 miles	8 hours

LIFT PRICES: (1993-94)
All Lifts Weekends (ages 7 to 61)
All Chairs $26
Beginner Chair only $22
Rope tow only $8
All Lifts Weekdays (ages 7 to 61)
Monday-Tuesday $12
Wednesday-Friday $16
Children 6 and under all days $5
(must be present when purchasing ticket)
Adults (62-69) Midweek and nights $12
                 Weekends (proof of age) $18
Seniors 70+ ski *free* (proof of age required)
Half-day tickets on sale at 1:00 pm
Night skiing begins at 5:00 pm

DAYS AND HOURS OF OPERATION:
Weekdays   9:30 am to 10:30 pm
Saturdays   9:00 am to 10:30 pm
Sundays and   9:00 am to 6:00 pm
CLOSED ON MONDAY
(except holiday Mondays, then open 9:30 am to 6:00 pm)

ALPENTAL INFORMATION AND FACILITIES:
RUNS   19
LIFTS   4 double chairs
              3 rope tows
              1 platter pull
FOOD   Two Day lodges with 2 cafeterias and 2 lounges
              (Beer Stube and Denny Mountain Lounge)
              Lodges are connected by a sky-walk.
AND MORE Rental/repair - alpine and snowboard
              Ski Shop- clothing, sunglasses, etc.
              Ski Check
              Ski School
              RV parking in lot (self-contained)

SNOWBOARDING:
Sometimes restricted by snow conditions. Check with the readerboard on the bridge crossing the creek.
Snowboard rentals

SPECIAL INFORMATION:
THE PASS: Alpental is one of four ski areas called "The Pass" at the summit of Snoqualmie Pass. These areas include Ski Acres, Snoqualmie, and Hyak. Tickets purchased at any of the four areas are good at the other three for the day.
SHUTTLE BUS: On weekends only, a *free* shuttle bus connects the four areas and runs on the half-hour.
CAUTION: The "back country" at Alpental is outside the designated ski area boundary and is difficult, hazardous and not regularly patrolled. The terrain is rugged and steep, and the danger of avalanches exists at all times. *OBEY ALL SIGNS RELATING TO THIS AREA.*
GUIDES: Guides are available to ski the back-country terrain; inquire at the ski school office or at Chair #17.
PASS CLOSURE: In very heavy snowfall conditions (one or more feet) the pass may be temporarily *CLOSED* by road maintenance for avalanche control. Be prepared to wait and carry chains.
SPECIAL ENTERTAINMENT: Live music in the "Beer Stube" on Friday and Saturday nights during peak season.

OVERNIGHT ACCOMMODATIONS:
SNOQUALMIE PASS

Best Western Summit Inn	1-800-528-1234
From Seattle	1-206-624-4040
	1-206-434-6300

NORTH BEND

Edgewick Inn	1-206-888-9000
North Bend Motel	1-206-888-1121

ISSAQUAH

Motel 6	1-206-392-8405
Holiday Inn	1-206-392-6421

CLE ELUM

Timber Lodge	1-509-674-5966
Cedar's Motel	1-509-674-5535
Chalet Motel	1-509-674-2320
Cle Elum Motel	1-509-674-5571
Stewart Lodge	1-509-674-4548
Moore House Bed and Breakfast	1-509-674-5939

BUSINESS ADDRESS:
Ski Lifts, Inc.
7900 SE 28th Street Suite 200
Mercer Island, WA 98040
(206) 232-8182

Courtesy of Armstrong Family. Photo by Joe Scalea.

SKI BLUEWOOD AREA

5,670' top elevation   **1,125' vertical drop**

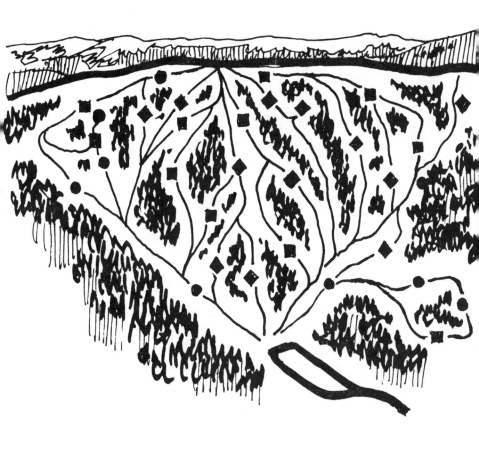

SKI BLUEWOOD

Bluewood is being discovered by more skiers each year. They advertise powder snow and lots of it and they don't lie! Because its location in the south eastern part of the state provides unique winter weather patterns, it has an average snowfall of 300 plus inches. The area first opened in 1979 and there are plans to add more runs with Forest Service approval in the near future. It is a family ski area as well as a collegiate one. Many Whitman college students take advantage of the one-hour drive that doesn't include a mountain pass. The Whitman collegiate race team trains here as well.

A friendly and affordable ski area, Bluewood caters to all winter snow seekers. It offers a half-pipe for snowboarders, backcountry runs through trees and down steep chutes, and a one-way ticket to the top of the mountain for cross country skiers. The winter sport of snowmobiling is available on a 25-mile snowmobile road that begins at the base of the ski area.

The nearby historic town of Dayton was the first county seat and is worth a visit during your ski trip. For history buffs, there is a walking tour of town (maps available in the restored Oregon Railroad depot, built in 1881). There are displays of railroad memorabilia, two historic districts to tour, the oldest courthouse in the state, antiques, and many photographs to generate your interest in this farming community.

For those who seek dining experiences as well as skiing experiences on their travels, try out the Patit Creek Restaurant. It is a "four star" restaurant. (Do make reservations; it is very popular.)

PHONE NUMBERS:

Snowline	(509) 382-2877
Information	(509) 382-4725
Ski School	(509) 382-4725

DIRECTIONS:

Bluewood is south of Colfax. Take Highway 26 to Dusty, then Highway 127, then Highway 12 to Dayton. At Dayton, follow signs to Bluewood (approximately 21.5 miles). Bluewood is north of Walla Walla on Highway 12 to Waitsburg, then to Dayton (approximately 52 miles).

DRIVING TIMES: (estimated)

Seattle	318 miles	6 hours
Portland	289 miles	5.5 hours
Spokane	150 miles	2.5 hours
Walla Walla	52 miles	1 hour
Dayton	22 miles	20 minutes
Tri-Cities	83 miles	1.5 hours
Boise	316 miles	6 hours

LIFT PRICES: (1993-94)

Adult $23
Child (8th grade and under) $18
Senior (over 65) $18
Student (with proof, high school and college) $20
Pre-school lift ticket (kindergarten and under)*free*
Half-day begins at 12:30 pm

DAYS AND HOURS OF OPERATION:

Weekdays   9:00 am to 4:00 pm
Saturday and Sunday   9:00 am to 4:00 pm
CLOSED Mondays in November and until December 21st
OPEN Mondays from December 21st to March 1st

BLUEWOOD INFORMATION AND FACILITIES:

RUNS	23 major runs (longest 2.25 miles)
LIFTS	2 triple chairs
	1 platter pull
FOOD	Day lodge with cafeteria and pub
AND MORE	Rental/repair- alpine and snowboard
	Ski Shop - accessories
	Ski School

SNOWBOARDING:
Half-pipe
Snowboard rentals

CROSS COUNTRY:
5 km of trail
Open Tuesday to Sunday
A $5 chair lift ride to the trail start or start at lodge.
Maps are available at the lodge.
There is no rental equipment for cross country.

SPECIAL INFORMATION:
POWDER SNOW: Bluewood is located in the Blue Mountain
range. Because of its unique location, there is very often
"powder dry" snow on the ski area.
TREE SKIING: There is tree skiing for **experts only**. It is
suggested that if you tree ski, be sure to ski with a friend for
safety.
BUS AND TRAIN: Walla Walla has a commercial airport and
is served by bus lines.
COLLEGE: Whitman College is in Walla Walla.

OVERNIGHT ACCOMMODATIONS:
On-mountain accommodations are not available.

DAYTON

Blue Mountain Coloial Inn	1-509-382-4076
Blue Mountain Motel	1-800-223-3366 or
	1-509-382-4724
Dayton Inn	1-509-382-5550
Inn at Dayton	1-509-382-4651

WAITSBURG

Waitsburg Motel	1-509-337-8103
Budget Motel	1-509-337-6412

WALLA WALLA

A and H Motel	1-509-529-0560
Best Western Pony Soldier	1-800-634-7669 or
	1-509-523-4360
Capri Motel	1-509-525-1130
City Center Motel	1-509-529-2660

Colonial Motel	1-509-529-1220
Comfort Inn Walla Walla	1-509-525-2522
Econo Lodge	1-509-529-4410
McFeeley Hotel	1-509-525-9792
Nendels Motor Inn	1-509-525-2200
Super 8	1-509-525-8800
Tapadera Motor Inn	1-509-525-2580
Walla Walla Travelodge	1-509-529-9940

COLFAX

Junction Motel	1-509-397-3403
Siesta Motel	1-509-397-3417
Wheel Inn Motel	1-509-397-3195

BUSINESS ADDRESS:

Ski Bluewood
PO Box 88
Dayton, WA 99328
(509) 382-4725

Courtesy of Jonas Roeser. Photo by Matt Woxland.

CRYSTAL MOUNTAIN AREA

7,000' top elevation   **3,100' vertical drop**

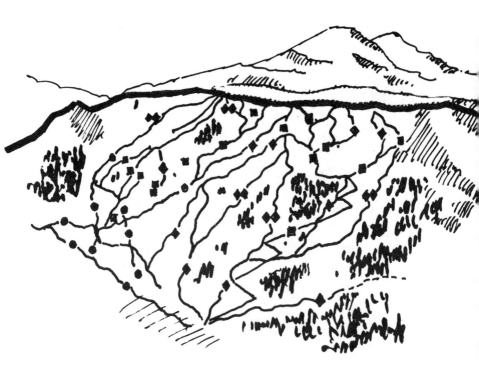

CRYSTAL MOUNTAIN

Crystal Mountain encourages destination skiing. It has overnight accommodations (three hotels and two condominium complexes) within walking distance of the ski area and is a popular week or weekend getaway. The area is developing gradually, with an emphasis on creating varied ski terrain, skier comforts and a village atmosphere.

The lodge is comfortable and offers many eating choices, from a brown bag area to cafeteria and restaurant seating. There is a deli and small grocery store with video rentals. Sunday church services are held in a beautiful chapel located to the left of the ticket area. Also available in the area are live entertainment, heated swimming pools, and a complete ski store with accessories, ski and snowboard equipment, and clothing.

Don't be discouraged by the huge parking lot or parking down the road from the ski area. You can drive up to an unloading zone right by the ticket area and then park your car, or take the *free* shuttle bus to the ticketing area from any parking area. If you prefer to walk (and warm up your legs), stay to the right in the parking lot and a trail will take you up to the ticket area.

Once on the mountain, the choice of terrain is up to you and your ability. Choose between easy beginner hills, or the more advanced bowls, bumps, back-country or giant slalom cruising runs. An express quad gets you to the top in just under five minutes.

Snowboarders now have a new area created to contain all the qualities they seek. Banks, rails and obstacles are all included in the snowboard park on the Quicksilver chairlift run.

Take the "Rainier Express" chair to the top to look in awe at Mt Rainier and enjoy the spectacular view of the Cascade Mountains. There is an excellent restaurant at the top here, and weather permitting, outside eating if you desire. What a view!

PHONE NUMBERS:

Snowline	**(206) 634-3771**
Information	**(206) 663-2265**
Ski School	**(206) 663-2265**
Disabled Lessons or Services	**(206) 663-2265**
Road Conditions	**(206) 455-7900**
	1-900-940-PASS (35¢)

DIRECTIONS:

Crystal is near Mt. Rainier. Driving south from Seattle on 1-5, take exit 142A to Auburn, then follow Highway 164 to Enumclaw. From Enumclaw take US 410 east for 33 miles to the Crystal Mountain Road turnoff.
Traveling north on 1-5 from Tacoma, take the exit to Enumclaw on Highway 410.
Coming west on 1-90, take the Auburn exit on Highway 18. Drive to Maple Valley, then go east on Highway 169 to Enumclaw.
Or on Highway 405, driving north or south, take Exit 4 to Renton/Enumclaw. Continue west through Maple Valley and then continue south on Highway 169 to Enumclaw.

DRIVING TIMES: (estimated)

Seattle	76 miles	1.5 hours
Tacoma	64 miles	1.5 hours
Portland	205 miles	4 hours
Tri-Cities	240 miles	5 hours
Enumclaw	33 miles	45 minutes

LIFT PRICES: (1993-94)

WEEKDAYS   Mon and Tues (ages 7-69) $15
Wed to Fri (ages 7-69) $19
Mon - Fri (6 and under and 70+) $5
(note: Special prices *not* in effect on holidays)
WEEKENDS   Adult (ages 18-61) $31
Student and Senior (ages 12-17 and 62-69) $26
Child (ages 7 -11) $19
All skiers 6 and under and over 70 $5
Half-day begins at 12:00 pm to 4:30 pm
Night skiing begins at 4:00 pm

DAYS AND HOURS OF OPERATION:

Weekdays   9:00 am to 4:30 pm
Sat - Sunday   8:30 am to 4:30 pm
Night skiing Fri, Sat, Sun, Christmas and Holidays
4:00 pm to 10:00 pm

CRYSTAL INFORMATION AND FACILITIES:

RUNS	29 major runs
LIFTS	3 triple chairs
	5 double chairs
	1 express quad
	1 regular quad
FOOD	Large modern day lodge at mountain base
	with cafeteria, lunchroom, pub,
	snack bar, restaurant and lounge
	Summit House on the mountain
AND MORE	Ski Shop - ski clothing, accessories and
	ski and snowboard equipment
	Snowmaking in base area
	Rental/repair- alpine and snowboard
	Ski School - See Special Information
	NASTAR racing or similar program in 1993-94
	SKI CHALLENGE coin-operated race course

Grocery store with video rentals.
Additional restaurants and entertainment in
Crystal ski area
Group accommodations and meeting facilities
RV parking in lot - 42 hook-ups available
Electricity, water and dump sites $10 a night

SNOWBOARDING:

New snowboard park area on Quicksilver with banks, rails and
obstacles. (1993-94)
Rentals and lessons

CHILD CARE:

(Located just prior to entering the parking lot to the right)
Plans are underway for 1993-94 season to have a child care
facility in the lodge.
Reservations recommended **(206) 663-2300**
Eight weeks to two years, midweek (non-holidays)
Infants two to seven years
8:30 am to 4:30 pm

CHURCH SERVICES: (Sunday)

Protestant 11:30 am
Catholic   12:30 pm

SPECIAL INFORMATION:

ROADS: From interstates, the roads to Crystal are two-lane. Don't get over anxious and try to pass, and observe the posted speed limits. The roads are well-patrolled. The last six miles has a very steep incline. In heavy snow conditions, it can require the use of chains or snow tires.

BUS IN AREA: There is a *free* shuttle bus from the parking lots to lifts.

BUS TO CRYSTAL: Crystal Mountain Express bus from Seattle to Crystal Mountain is available seven days a week. Call **(206) 626-5208** for information, prices, and pick-up locations in Seattle, Bellevue, Renton, and Auburn.

DISABLED SKIERS: Ski lessons are private lessons only and are limited to a mono-ski program. The lodge is equipped with an elevator, and the lavatories are designed for wheelchair access.

CROSS COUNTRY SKIING: The closest area is in Greenwater, a Washington State Park, which has groomed runs available; inquire Forest Service **(206) 825-6585**.

SKIKEY: This is an electronic ticket introduced by Crystal in the 1993-94 season, which tracks your vertical feet skied. Designed for the frequent skier, it allows you a special gate at all lifts, a vertical feet readout, prizes, and messaging and finder services. (See Willamette Pass ski area, page 167.)

OVERNIGHT ACCOMMODATIONS:

CRYSTAL MOUNTAIN

Central Reservation for area	1-800-852-1444
Silver Skis Chalet Condo	1-206-663-2558
Quicksilver Lodge	1-206-663-2558
Village Inn Hotel	1-206-663-2558
Alpine Inn Hotel	1-206-663-2262
Crystal Chalet Condo	1-206-663-2558

ALTA

Alta Crystal Resort	1-206-663-2500

ENUMCLAW

Ridge Motel	1-206-825-6352
Lee's Restaurant and Hotel	1-206-825-3161

BUSINESS ADDRESS:

Crystal Mountain Resort
1 Crystal Mountain Boulevard
Crystal Mountain, WA 98022 **(206) 663-2265**

Courtesy of Crystal Mountain.

49° NORTH AREA

5,773' top elevation   **1,900' vertical drop**

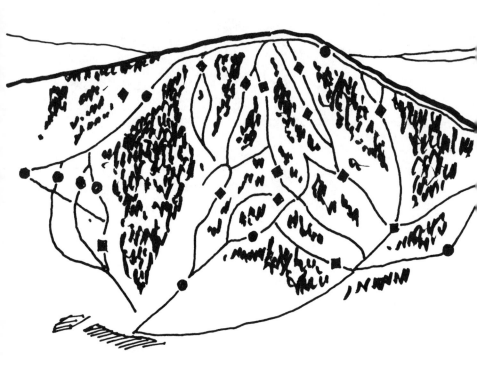

49° NORTH

Too often overlooked by traveling skiers, 49° North is only an hour's easy drive from Spokane. The town of Chewelah is a small logging town and has limited (but nice) accommodations. The ski area offers an interesting combination of bumps, groomed runs and "powder skiing," On the right day, the skiing can be exceptional.

The area attracts a wide variety of skiers from Spokane and smaller communities. The runs are well groomed and the beginner slopes are excellent. Skiers vary from families (there is a nice nursery for toddlers) to college students and senior skiers.

The area strives to accommodate many interests with its varied terrain and offers a wide selection of lessons for all abilities. Snowboarders are attracted by this area's permanent half-pipe and radical runs. For the cross country family, there are also 15 km of groomed trails with skating lanes and tracks. For the adventurous, there is plenty of back-country skiing terrain.

The lodge is comfortable and has huge windows which frame the slopes. Weather permitting, there is an immense deck for outside eating (used mostly in the spring). The 1993-94 season will unfold the extensive remodeling to the ski shop, cafeteria and restroom facilities.

In the spring there are some fun events. One is "Yosemite Sam Days," which includes games, drawings and races. Another is "Oyster Days," with oyster eating and skiing competitions.

But the best news is that there are seldom lift lines at this conveniently located area.

PHONE NUMBERS:

Information	**(509) 935-6649**
Snowline	**(509) 458-9208**
Ski School	**(509) 935-6649**

DIRECTIONS:

49° North is about an hour's drive (52 miles) north of Spokane on Highway 395.

From Spokane, (going east or west on I-90) take the exit to Colville, Highway 395, which will put you on Division Street North. Keep to the right, the street is one-way and then becomes two-way. Drive to Chewelah, and in the center of town, turn right at the directional sign on Main Street. Then continue ten more miles to the ski area. There is only one more sign to direct you: it says "Chewelah Ski Area."

DRIVING TIMES: (estimated)

Chewelah	10 miles	20 minutes
Spokane	52 miles	1 hour
Seattle	332 miles	6 hours
Portland	414 miles	7.5 hours
Boise	477 miles	9 hours

LIFT PRICES: (1993-94)

WEEKENDS (Sat -Sun)
>   Adult (18-62) $23
>   Junior (7-15) $15
>   Student (16+ college students, ID required) $18
>   Senior (62-70) $18

WEEKDAYS (Mon, Tues and Fri)
>   Adult $17
>   Junior $12
>   Student $15
>   Senior $15

ID required for student, junior and senior tickets
Children 6 and under, Adults 70 and over ski *free*
Half-day begins at 12:30 pm

DAYS AND HOURS OF OPERATION:

OPEN 9:00 am to 4:00 pm Monday, Tuesday, Friday, Saturday and Sunday
CLOSED Wednesday and Thursday except holiday periods
Three ticket sessions: 9:00 am to 1:00 pm, 9:00 am to 4:00 pm and 12:30 pm to 4:00 pm
Season ends around April 4th

49° NORTH INFORMATION AND FACILITIES:

RUNS   21 major runs
LIFTS   4 double chairs
FOOD   Day lodge with cafeteria and "Boomtown Bar"
AND MORE   Rental/repair-alpine and snowboard
              Ski Shop - accessories
              Ski School
              RV parking in lot (self-contained)

SNOWBOARDING:
Half-pipe
Snowboard rentals

CROSS COUNTRY:
15 km of trails (*free*)
(Limited rentals available, call to reserve)

CHILD CARE:
Two months and older
Reservations required **(509) 935-6649** ext 118
Toddler reservations recommended
Complimentary mid-week day care on Monday,
Tuesday and Friday (except Holidays)

SPECIAL INFORMATION:
SKI AREA RENTAL: The entire ski area is available for your
organization or company to rent on Friday nights.
CHILD CARE: For children in lessons there is a special
"Noontime Connection" which includes child care and lunch.
EATING: Barbecue on the deck, weather permitting.

OVERNIGHT ACCOMMODATIONS:
49° (privately owned "Loop Hole" Condominiums)

CHEWELAH
49er Motel   1-509-935-8613
Nordlig Motel   1-509-935-6704

SPOKANE
See Mount Spokane listings, page 60.

BUSINESS ADDRESS:
49° North
PO Box 166
Chewelah, WA 99109
(509) 935-6649

Courtesy of 49° North.

HYAK SKI AREA

3,745' top elevation   **1,145' vertical drop**

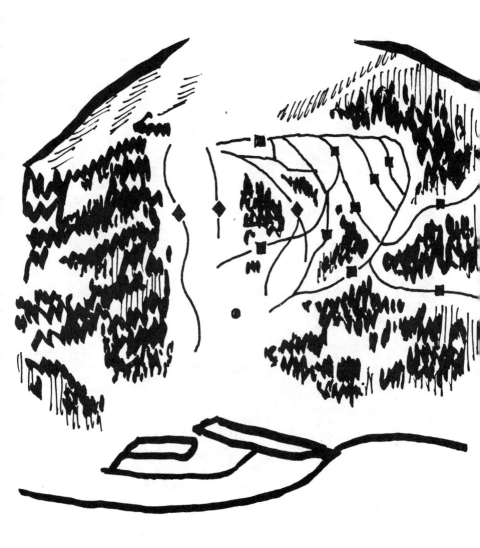

HYAK

This area has survived many ownerships in the past years. In 1992 it became part of the Snoqualmie/Ski Acres/Alpental operations, assuring its future availability for those who have long enjoyed its slopes.

Open on a limited operation schedule, Hyak is part of the Snoqualmie Pass operations, which gives the ticket buyer the bonus of being able to ski any or all of the other three ski areas in the same day. No need to move your car; there is a bus on the weekends which connects all the areas.

The selection of runs from the top of the chair, although limited in number, offers a variety of several tree lined runs that drop from "Milwaukii Ridge." There are two open faces to test your skills and a gentle beginner area with its own chairlift near the base of the area.

There is something for everyone here. The area has a continuous drop of over 1,000 vertical feet and includes a half-pipe for snowboarders, and access to the Mt Catherine Loop cross country ski tour.

Several ski schools operate here on the weekends, in addition to the resident school.

PHONE NUMBERS:

Snowline	(206) 236-1600
Information	(206) 434-SNOW
Ski School	(206) 434-6400
Hyak Cross Country Center	(206) 434-6646

DIRECTIONS:
Hyak is at the eastern end of the four area ski facilities at the summit of Snoqualmie Pass and is accessible off Exit 54 or from Exit 53. Continue driving east on SR 906, past Snoqualmie and Ski Acres areas.

DRIVING TIMES:
See Alpental section, page 18.

LIFT PRICES:
See Alpental section, page 18.

DAYS AND HOURS OF OPERATION:
Friday Night   5:00 pm to 10:30 pm
Saturday, Sunday and Holidays* 9:00 am to 6:00 pm
(*Martin Luther King Day and Presidents' Day)
OPEN December 26 through March 14 only.

HYAK INFORMATION AND FACILITIES:
RUNS	13
LIFTS	3 double chairs (not all operating)
FOOD	Day lodge with cafeteria and lounge
AND MORE	Rental/repair-alpine and snowboard
	Ski School
	Ski Shop (accessories)
	RV parking in lot (self-contained)

SNOWBOARDING:
Half-pipe
Snowboard rentals

SPECIAL INFORMATION:
CROSS COUNTRY: You have access the Mt. Catherine Loop, which is a cross country ski tour from Hyak.
SHUTTLE BUS: On weekends, there is a free bus which connects this area to Snoqualmie, Ski Acres and Alpental.

BUSINESS ADDRESS:
Ski Lifts, Inc.
7900 SE 28th Street Suite 200
Mercer Island, WA 98040
(206) 232-8182

Courtesy of SKIFORALL. Photo by Johna Peterson.

MISSION RIDGE AREA

6,700' top elevation   **2,140' vertical drop**

MISSION RIDGE

Mission Ridge is evolving into a convenient weekend getaway for many skiers from west of the Cascades. In 1992, new owners made some dramatic changes which contribute to a pleasant skiing experience.

The lodge has been expanded and a new kitchen/serving area has been designed. (However, even with the expansion, it's wise to avoid the noon-hour rush.) The menu includes a roast beef sandwich, which is often the preferred item. And, especially for those "west side" latte´ lovers, there is an espresso cart!

The services and lessons for children are exceptional. There is a *free* rope tow and mini-hill at the base of the area near the lodge, for children and adults who are not quite ready to ride a chairlift. The child care area is bright and well staffed. The "Kids Club" ski school can include lessons, lunch, ski equipment and supervision. Everything is planned to ensure a pleasant introduction and day of skiing for the younger travelers.

The mountain layout offers a great selection of dynamic runs carved through the trees. They are varied and challenging (with about 60% for intermediates), and well-groomed to a corduroy texture. Mid-mountain, snowboarders have their own area, complete with half-pipe and a rope tow.

From the lifts and hills, the view down to the Columbia River Valley is spectacular, as is the view from the top of the ridge to the South. On a clear day you can see Mount Stuart, Mount Rainier, Mount St Helens, and even Mount Hood in Oregon.

Back in town, The Windmill restaurant is one the best steak houses in Wenatchee. A new family restaurant and tavern with live entertainment and micro brews, is McGlenn's. There are a wide variety of accommodations, movie theaters, and a city ice rink for after-ski family entertainment. Or drive to Leavenworth (about a half-hour away) for a "Bavarian Village" experience.

PHONE NUMBERS:

Information	**(509)-663-7631**
Snowline	**(509)-663-3200** or
	1-800-374-1693

DIRECTIONS:

Mission Ridge is 13 miles south of Wenatchee. Prominent signs direct you on S/285 through the business section (it is one-way) to the east end of Wenatchee. Just prior to crossing the Columbia River to East Wenatchee, keep right and continue on Mission Street. The road becomes Squilchuck Road, then keeping right, it becomes Mission Ridge Road. The road is two lanes and can be icy in the early morning hours. It winds up a canyon lined with orchards, and then becomes more mountainous as it approaches the ski area. Drive with caution.

DRIVING TIMES: (estimated)

Seattle	155 miles	3 hours
Spokane	165 miles	3+ hours
Wenatchee	13 miles	25 minutes
Portland	203 miles	6 hours
Tri-Cities	134 miles	3 hours

LIFT PRICES: (1993-94)

Monday through Friday **SPECIAL PRICE** all ages $13
Saturday and Sunday and Holidays:
Adult $26
Youth (7-15) $14
Student (16-20 or with college ID) $18
Children under 6 ski *free*
Seniors 62+ and active military with ID $18
Two half-day sessions on weekends:
        8:30 am to 12:30 pm
        12:00 pm to 4:00 pm
(These sessions affect the parking situation)
Night skiing begins at 4:00 pm
Night skiing on Thurs, Fri, Sat, and holidays
Special night skiing price of $6.00 for all ages

DAYS AND HOURS OF OPERATION:

Monday to Wednesday	9:00 am to 4:00 pm
Thursday and Friday	9:00 am to 10:00 pm

Saturday, Sunday and Holidays open at 8:30 am
Night skiing Saturday until 10:00 pm

MISSION RIDGE INFORMATION AND FACILITIES:

RUNS	30
LIFTS	4 double chairs
	Free rope tow for beginners at the base
	Rope tow mid-mountain for snowboarding
FOOD	Day lodge with cafeteria and beerstube
	Snack Shack on mid-mountain
	Lodge on mid-mountain
AND MORE	Rental/repair-alpine and snowboard
	Ski Shop
	Ski School
	RV parking in lot (self-contained)
	Snowmaking
	Free ski check
	Free parking lot shuttle

SNOWBOARDING:

Half-pipe area with its own rope tow
Rentals and lessons

CHILD CARE:

Infant to six years (Excellent facilities)
8:00 am to 4:00 pm weekdays
8:00 am to 10:00 pm Thurs, Fri, Sat and holidays
Reservations **1-509-663-7631**

SPECIAL INFORMATION:

WIND: When the wind is blowing, Mission Ridge can be extremely cold. Pack extra clothing and layer for warmth.
PARKING: If you arrive later in the day to ski, and the cars are parked down the road, it is worth a trip up through the parking lot to find a vacant spot left by a half-day skier. (Most times, we found an empty space or at least were able to drop off the ski gear in the drop off area in the lower lot.)
BUS: There is a *free* shuttle service in the area.
SKI LINK: Bus service is offered from Wenatchee to Mission Ridge. It runs daily and stops at Park and Rides at the Orchard Inn, the Wenatchee Convention Center, in East Wenatchee at the Four Seasons Inn, and at Lincoln Park. For information and a map call **1-800-851-LINK** or **509-662-1155**.

KIDS CLUB: Kids Club is a unique approach which combines day care and skiing for children ages 4 to 12, and also provides rental equipment. This area is outstanding in its accommodations for young skiers.

LIFT TICKET: You can receive a 20% lift ticket discount when presenting a current seasons pass from another ski area.

SAMPLE SKIING: "Taste before you ski" allows you to sample the skiing (with ticket purchase) for the first hour and receive credit for another day or for purchases in the gift shop if the conditions fail to meet your expectations.

COMMERCIAL TRANSPORTATION: Wenatchee is on regularly scheduled airplane, train and bus service.

OVERNIGHT ACCOMMODATIONS:

WENATCHEE

Central Reservations (out of state)	1-509-996-2148
Central Reservations (WA state)	1-800-422-3048
Avenue Motel	1-509-663-7161
Chieftan Motel	1-509-572-4456
Holiday Lodge	1-800-722-0852
Lyle's Motel	1-800-582-3788
Orchard Inn	1-800-368-4571
Scotty's Motel	1-800-235-8165
Starlite Motel	1-509-663-8115
Uptowner Motel	1-800-288-5279
Welcome Inn	1-509-663-7121
Westcoast Wenatchee	1-800-426-0670
Best Western Heritage Inn	1-800-664-6565

EAST WENATCHEE

Red Lion Inn	1-800-547-8010
Rivers Inn	1-800-922-3199
Four Seasons Inn	1-800-223-6611

(also Leavenworth, listed under Steven's Pass, and Lake Chelan are close enough to commute.)

BUSINESS ADDRESS:

Mission Ridge
P O Box 1668
Wenatchee, WA 98807-1668
(509) 663-6543

Centennial Games at Mission Ridge.

MOUNT BAKER SKI AREA

5,050' top elevation   **1,500' vertical drop**

MOUNT BAKER

Mount Baker has the earliest season opening of the Washington areas, and has an average snowfall of 750 inches. Skiers rush here as soon as the opening is announced to try out their new gear and old legs! The area is attractive to Canadian skiers, collegiates, military, families, young adults, seniors, snowboarders and snowplayers.

One of the first ski areas to allow snowboarding, Mt Baker is now host to many competitions. One of these is the "Banked Slalom" in January. It is also host to a variety of additional events which include a telemark race, mogul competition, and an amateur speed skiing competition. They have a convenient event hot line for all activities. Call **206-734-2050** for updated information.

It's hard to ski without being a little in awe of the surrounding dormant volcanoes of Mt Shuskan and Mt Baker. The ski area is carved out between these two looming giants. The history and development of this area makes interesting reading. Dating back to the 1800's when gold was discovered here, the area has always held a special appeal to skiers, hikers and outdoor enthusiasts.

The chair lifts are well placed to connect the two base areas, depositing skiers at the tops of the multitude of runs. These include open intermediate runs, chutes, and through-the-trees-and over-the-bumps black diamonds. The lower slopes, nearer the lodges, are gently rolling for beginner skiing. This area also has the qualities that snowboarders seek: natural rolls, obstacles, wind lips and natural half-pipes.

When skiing here, I'm sure you'll notice the run names such as "Nose Dive, Sticky Wicket, Honkers, and Oh Zone." Makes you wonder just who thought up these whimsical names...

PHONE NUMBERS:

Snowline	**(206) 671-0221**
Information	**(206) 734-6671**
Ski School	**(206) 592-5550**
Road Conditions	**(206) 455-7900**
	1-900-PASS (35¢)
Ski Report (from Canada)	**(604) 688-1595**

DIRECTIONS:

Mount Baker is 56 miles east of Bellingham on State Route 542-A. Traveling north or south on I-5, take Exit 255 to Mount Baker. The road is two-lane all the way and requires headlights for safety and cautious driving. Be prepared for icy conditions especially in the morning.

DRIVING TIMES: (estimated)

Seattle	143 miles	2.5 hours
Portland	318 miles	5.5 hours
(in good conditions)		
Bellingham	56 miles	1+ hours
Glacier	17 miles	25 minutes

LIFT PRICES: (1993-94)

WEEKENDS	Adults (16 and older)	$26
	Youth (7 to 15 with proof)	$19
	Seniors (60-69) $19	
MIDWEEK	Adults $17	
	Youth $12	
	Seniors $12	

Children under 6 and Adults over 70 ski *free*
(Mid-week prices effective only on non-holidays.)
Half-day begins 12:30 pm
No night skiing

DAYS AND HOURS OF OPERATION:

This schedule is different from any other ski area listed. If you are not familiar with the operations, be sure to call to assure that the mountain is open.

Generally the mountain is OPEN:
Monday, Thursday and Friday 9:00 am to 3:30 pm
Weekends and holidays   8:30 am to 3:30 pm
CLOSED Tuesdays and Wednesdays in January, February, March, and April.
OPEN the entire third week of March and first week of April.

MT BAKER INFORMATION AND FACILITIES:

RUNS 31

LIFTS 6 double chairs
1 rope tow
2 quads (not high speed)

FOOD Upper Base area: day lodge with cafeteria,
deli and taproom
Snack bar on mountain at base of Chair 4
and 5 (Razorhone Cafe)
Snack bar at lower lot - limited to machine
service for drinks and snacks

AND MORE NASTAR
RV parking in southeast corner of upper lot
(self-contained)
Ski School
Snowplay area at the upper base area
Rental/repair - alpine and snowboard

SNOWBOARDING:

Natural half-pipes and rolls, obstacles, and wind lips.
Rentals and lessons

CHILD CARE:

Children two years + (toilet trained)
Located in the lodge at upper base area
Weekends and holidays only
Reservations suggested **(206) 734-6771**

SPECIAL INFORMATION:

LOCATION: Mount Baker ski area is actually located between
Mount Shuksan (9,720') and Mount Baker (10, 750').

ROAD CAUTION: The road from Bellingham is two lanes and
requires cautious driving. Watch for icy patches in the
mornings, especially in shaded areas.

SKIER CAUTION: *Many of the runs converge with each other,
and it is important to check the upper slope before merging into
traffic.*

GROUPS: Groups of 20 or more are offered special rates with a
one week advance notice required.

TRANSPORTATION: Bellingham is served by bus lines and
has a commercial airport.

COLLEGE: Bellingham the home of Western Washington University and has a good selection of accommodations.
HOT LINE: Area Hot line for events **206-734-2050**.
CURRENCY: Canadian Currency is accepted and dependent on current exchange rate.
INFORMATION: Complete information about the Mt Baker ski area is presented in the *Mt Baker Experience*, available from Magnuson Enterprises, 1740 Electric, Bellingham, WA, 98226. It has an excellent map of the road to Mt Baker with all the attractions and places to stay and eat clearly marked.

OVERNIGHT ACCOMMODATIONS:
GLACIER:

Glacier Creek Motel	
(cabins and motel)	1-206-599-2991
Snowline Inn Condo	1-206-599-2788
The Logs (cabins)	1-206-599-2711
Mt Baker Chalet (cabins)	1-206-599-2405
Mt Baker Cabin Rentals	1-206-599-2453
Snowline Inn Hotel	1-206-599-2788 or
	1-800-228-0119

BELLINGHAM:

Coachman Inn	1-206-671-9000
Pony Soldier	1-206-734-8830
Travel Lodge	1-206-734-1900
Best Western Heritage Inn	1-206-674-1912
Bell Motel	1-206-733-2520
Ramada	1-206-734-8830
Park Motel	1-206-733-8280
Motel 6	1-206-671-4494
Lakeway Inn (Best Western)	1-206-671-1011

BUSINESS ADDRESS:
Mount Baker Ski Area
1017 Iowa Street
Bellingham, WA 98226
(206) 734-6771

Mount Baker lodge.

MOUNT SPOKANE AREA

6,000' top elevation   **2,100' vertical drop**

MOUNT SPOKANE

Mount Spokane is conveniently close to Spokane (only 27 miles), and is popular to a variety of people who seek a day, weekend or even just a few hours on the slopes. There are condominiums available within a short driving distance of the ski area. However, plan to bring your supplies, as there are no grocery stores, etc. in the area.

This area may not have the fanciest of lodges, but it has the most affordable ticket in the state! The runs are wide and long and generally would be rated intermediate. Pack your giant slalom skis here for the ultimate ski experience. If you like tree skiing, there are some excellent areas to test your skills, as well as mid-run mogul fields to keep you flexible. Be sure to try out the shuttle bus between lodges. It is a new experience in transportation.

Just a little way down the mountain there are groomed snowmobile trails and cross country trails. This entire area is all part of the Mt Spokane State Park, which makes it unique to all the Northwest ski areas.

If you are staying in Spokane, there are a variety of after ski activities which can include the public ice rinks, an IMAX theater, the world famous Looff Carrousel (a US Historical Landmark), sleigh rides/hay rides at the Trail Town Stables, winery tours, concerts, etc. All can add to your ski trip adventure.

PHONE NUMBERS:

Information	**(509) 238-6281**
Snowline	**(509) 239-6223**
Ski School	**(509) 238-6281**

DIRECTIONS:

Mt Spokane is about 30 miles north of Spokane. Exit from I-90 in Spokane on Division Street (Highway 395). Keeping in the right lanes, you will travel about four miles on a busy city street. You will exit right on Highway 2 to Newport. After about a mile on Highway 2, you will exit to Mt Spokane State Park on Highway 206. There are *NO* signs which say "Mt Spokane Ski Area," so follow the Mount Spokane State Park signs there.

DRIVING TIMES: (estimated)

Spokane	30 miles	45 minutes
Seattle	340 miles	6 hours
Portland	444 miles	8 hours
Boise	416 miles	7.5 hours

LIFT PRICES: (1992-93)

WEEKDAYS   Adults $15
WEEKENDS   Adults $2
ALL DAYS   Child (8-12) $15
Children 7 and under ski *free*
Half-day begins at 12:00 pm

DAYS AND HOURS OF OPERATION:

Wednesday - Saturday 9:00 am to 10:00 pm
Sunday   9:00 am to   4:00 pm
CLOSED Monday and Tuesday (except Holidays)
Night skiing begins at 4:00 pm

MOUNT SPOKANE INFORMATION AND FACILITIES:

RUNS	35 major trails
LIFTS	5 double chairs
FOOD	2 day lodges
	#1 operated by Forest Service
	#2 operated by ski area
	2 cafeterias
	(#1 limited service, #2 full service and Lounge)
AND MORE	Rental/repair- alpine and snowboard
	Ski Shop - accessories
	Ski School
	RV parking in lot (self-contained)

SNOWBOARDING:
No half-pipe
Snowboard rentals

SPECIAL INFORMATION:
ROAD CAUTION: Highway 206 from Spokane is a two-lane road and has a steep climb with frost heaves for about the last eight miles. The speed limit is 15 to 35 mph.
WEEKDAY SERVICES: On weekdays, drive to the second lodge for services and tickets.
LOCKERS: There are day lockers in both lodges for gear storage.
RENTAL SHOP: Look for an improved rental shop and service in 1993-94. "Snow Runners" are available for rental.
SNO-PARK AREA: There is a Sno-Park area about one mile from the ski area for snowmobiling.
KIRK'S LODGE: At Kirk's Lodge there are snowmobile and cross country rentals and trails. There is also a snowplay and sledding area and RV hook-ups here. (See Kirk's Lodge below.)
BUS: Free shuttle bus from lodge to lodge on the weekends. (You have to see this "bus.")
LODGE: The spectacular building to the right of the main lodge is the National Ski Patrol lodge.
SKI SHOP: There are some "unique" locally made ski hats available.
COMMERCIAL TRANSPORTATION: Spokane has regularly scheduled airline, train and bus services.
COLLEGE: Gonzaga University and Eastern Washington University are in the Spokane area.

OVERNIGHT ACCOMMODATIONS:
MT SPOKANE

Snowblaze Condominiums	1-509-238-4630
Kirk's Lodge	1-509-238-9114

SPOKANE
(this is just a partial listing , selected because they are closest to Mt Spokane and Chewelah)

Apple Tree Inn Motel	1-800-353-5796
Quality Inn - Oakwood	1-509-767-5151
Best Western Trade Winds	1-509-326-5500
Liberty Motel	1-509-467-6000

Comfort Inn	1-509-467-7111
Royal Scot Motel	1-509-467-6672
Cavanaugh's River Inn	1-800-THE-INNS
Day's Inn	1-509-926-5399
Spokane Convention and Visitors Bureau	
for more area listings	1-509-724-1341

BUSINESS ADDRESS:

Mount Spokane Skiing Corporation
P O Box 159
Mead, WA 99021
(509) 938-7575

Set up for a race at Mt Spokane.

SKI ACRES AREA

3,900' top elevation   **1,040' vertical drop**

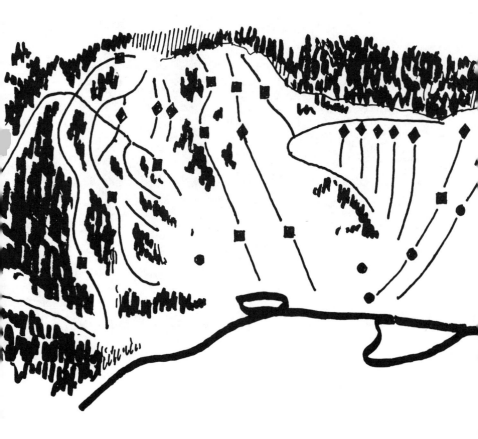

SKI ACRES

Ski Acres, with its multiple-level terrain, offers runs for the novice to the advanced skier. There are gentle beginner slopes, short steep side-hill runs, and excellent short mogul fields. Adding to the variety are longer tree-lined runs, which take you top to bottom. There are several opportunities to cut over to other runs on the hill from these longer runs, allowing you to design your own combination and adding a new challenge each time down.

Snowboarders, who delight in the natural runs, and young skiers, who like to experiment with skiing styles, gather here to try out their skills. The area is also attractive to many "snowplay" families who come to use the Snowflake tubing area. It also has cross country ski trails which begin with a chairlift ride or a walk from the Cross Country Center. The design of this cross country center is, appropriately, a log cabin. It has a very cozy and homey feeling, and provides a waxing area, deli, ski accessories and rentals.

The area management has done a nice job of incorporating a variety of snow activities, giving each its own locale, yet keeping all areas accessible from the main parking lot.

In the summer, from late June to the end of September, the Cross Country Center becomes the Mountain Bike and Hiking Center, offering rentals and instruction. The Silver Fir triple chairlift provides transportation for biker and bike (or for fisherman, hiker, photographer, etc.) The deli bar is open with sandwiches or picnics to go.

PHONE NUMBERS:

Information	(206) 434-SNOW
Snowline	(206) 236-1600
Ski School	(206) 823-2690 or
	(206) 434-6400
Lodge	(206) 434-6671

DIRECTIONS:
Ski Acres is part of the four area complex at the summit of Snoqualmie Pass called THE PASS.
Traveling east or west on 1-90, it is on the east side of the summit, accessible from Exit 53 or 54.

DRIVING TIMES:
See Alpental Section, page 18.

LIFT PRICES:
See Alpental Section, page 18.

DAYS AND HOURS OF OPERATION:
Saturday	9:00 am to 10:30 pm
Sunday	9:00 am to 9:00 pm
Monday	9:00 am to 10:30 pm
Wednesday to Friday	9:00 am to 10:30 pm

CLOSED Tuesdays, except Holiday Tuesdays
Half-day begins at 1:00 pm

SKI ACRES INFORMATION AND FACILITIES:
RUNS	15
LIFTS	6 double chairs
	2 triple chairs
	5 rope tows
FOOD	Day lodge with cafeteria and beerstube
AND MORE	Ski Shop - accessories
	Ski School
	Rental/repair-alpine and snowboard
	RV parking in lot (self-contained)

SNOWBOARDING:
Very popular area with natural rolls
Snowboard rentals

CHILD CARE:
Toddler : One to two and a half years and up
Reservations required **206-434-6406**

SKI ACRES and HYAK CROSS COUNTRY CENTER:

INFORMATION: (206) 434-SNOW
SNOWLINE: (206) 236-1600
DIRECTIONS: From Ski Acres alpine area travel east one and a quarter mile to the Cross Country Center.
PARKING: Limited parking for early birds! General parking is available on the highway or in the large lot at Ski Acres.
TRAILS: 55 km of trails (4 km lighted for night skiing)
SERVICES: Nordic Retail Shop
  Ski School
  Trailside cafe and deli
  Public waxing area
  Rentals
TRACK USE PRICES: (1993-94)
Children 5 and under *free*
Youth (6 - 14) $4 lower trail $8 upper trail
Adult (15 - 61) $5 lower trail $9 upper trail
Senior (62+) $4 lower trail $8 upper trail
(Includes two round-trip chairlift rides to trail start and use of the Hyak and Mt Catherine trail system)

HOURS AND DAYS OF OPERATION:
Monday, Wed to Fri   9:30 am to 5:00 pm
CLOSED Tuesdays
Saturday - Sunday   9:00 am to 5:00 pm
Nights: Wed to Sat   5:00 pm to 10:00 pm

SNOWFLAKE TUBING AND SNOWPLAY AREA:

INFORMATION: (206) 434-6443
DIRECTIONS: located at the east end of the main parking lot
        at Ski Acres
HOURS:
    Friday   11:00 am to 10:00 pm
    Saturday   9:00 am to 10:00 pm
    Sunday/Holidays 9:00 am to 5:00 pm
    Mondays   11:00 am to 5:00 pm
    OPEN Friday to Monday, holidays, and holiday
    Mondays
    CLOSED Tuesday, Wednesday and Thursday
ROPE TOWS: 4 rope tows
RENTALS: Tube rentals-regular and truck tubes available

FOOD: Snack bar
PASS PRICES: Day Pass $6.50 all ages
(Groups of 25 or more $5.50)
Children under 5 with an adult *free*
*BE SURE TO PICK UP A BROCHURE WHICH INCLUDES
SAFETY TIPS ON TUBING.*

SPECIAL INFORMATION:
THE PASS INFORMATION: See Alpental section for
information general to all four areas.
SKI TRAIL: Ski trail links Ski Acres to Snoqualmie area.
SUMMER ACTIVITIES: Summer Mountain Bike and Hiking
Center offers bike rentals and chairlift transportation to the
mountain trail systems. **(206) 434-6646**
SHUTTLE BUS: Weekend shuttle bus between Summit Inn and
the four ski areas for clients.

OVERNIGHT ACCOMMODATIONS:
See Alpental section

BUSINESS ADDRESS:
Ski Lifts Inc.
7900 SE 28th Street Suite 200
Mercer Island, WA 98040
(206) 232-8182

Courtesy of Ski Lifts Inc. Photo by Kelly O'neil.

SNOQUALMIE SKI AREA

3,900' top elevation　　　　　　　　　　　**900' vertical drop**

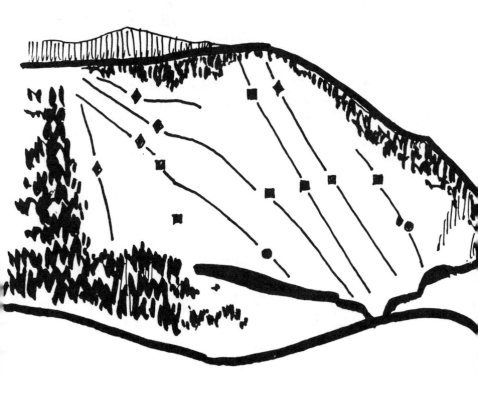

SNOQUALMIE

If you are learning to ski, Snoqualmie is quite possibly the best choice of the four ski areas at the summit. The area even advertises that it is "where most people from Seattle learned to ski." From one rope tow, built in 1937, to the nine chairlifts and two rope tows of today, this area has echoed the overall growth of the greater Seattle area.

The slopes are perfect for teaching and learning. Many ski schools offer programs here on weekends, in addition to the resident ski school. Several junior and senior racing programs, in addition to NASTAR, train and compete here. SKIFORALL, an alpine and nordic ski instruction program for people with disabilities, is also centered here. Whatever your skiing ability or needs, the runs are great for practicing your skills and building your confidence.

Closest accommodations are at The Summit Inn (Best Western), which is within walking distance from the slopes and has a heated indoor pool, cable TV, and restaurant. This addition to the area has made it a popular destination.

In recent years *SKI* magazine rated Snoqualmie "number one in accessibility to a major population." Travel is on a four-lane divided interstate from east and west, making it a convenient drive, whether for a few hours, a day, night, or weekend of skiing.

PHONE NUMBERS:

Information	**(206) 434-SNOW**
Snowline	**(206) 236-1600**
Lodge	**(206) 434-6161**
Ski School	**(206) 434-6363**

DIRECTIONS:
Snoqualmie is one of four ski areas at the Summit of Snoqualmie Pass on I-90. Exits 52, 53, or 54 will take you to Snoqualmie.

DRIVING TIMES:
See Alpental Section, page 18.

LIFT PRICES:
See Alpental Section, page 18.

DAYS AND HOURS OF OPERATION:
OPEN Tuesday to Sunday 9:00 am - 10:30 pm
CLOSED Mondays except Holiday Mondays

SNOQUALMIE INFORMATION AND FACILITIES:

RUNS	11
LIFTS	2 triple chairs
	1 quad
	6 double chairs
	2 rope tows
FOOD	3 day lodges
	Alpenhaus Lodge - Webb's Bar and Grill and cafeteria
	Slide In Lodge - tavern and cafeteria
	Thunderbird Lodge-cafeteria on mountain
AND MORE	Ski School
	Ski Shop - accessories
	2 rental/repair -alpine and snowboard
	NASTAR racing **(206) 434-6363**
	RV parking in lot (self-contained)

SNOWBOARDING:
Half-pipe to left of 360 Bowl Area
Snowboard rentals

CHILD CARE:
Toddler and up (in house to left of lodge)
Reservations recommended
(206) 434-6254

CHURCH SERVICES:

Sundays at St Bernard's Chapel
Protestant Service   10:30 am
Catholic Service   12:00 pm

SPECIAL INFORMATION:

TERRAIN: Snoqualmie is the perfect terrain for beginner and intermediate skiing.

SKI SCHOOLS: It is a "Mecca" for ski schools, racing programs, and the SKIFORALL Foundation.

SKI SPECIALS: There are Parent-Tot ski specials during the week.

GROUPS: Accommodations for large groups, parties and rentals are available.

BUS: I-90 SKI BUS service from Seattle, Bellevue and Issaquah to Snoqualmie Pass.

Reservations **(206) 434-6363**.

ENTERTAINMENT: Live music in Slide In Lounge on Friday and Saturday evenings.

AREA SERVICES: There is a service station at the summit area which also has a grocery store, deli, video rentals, and an ATM machine. A traveler's rest stop is nearby.

RESTAURANT: There is also a Pancake House restaurant located in the Summit Inn.

INFORMATION CENTER: The National Forest Service has a staffed information center and provides a wide resource of information for all travelers.

For more information general to the four-area ski facilities at Snoqualmie, refer to the Alpental section.

TRAIL: Connecting ski trail between Snoqualmie and Ski Acres.

DISABLED SERVICES: Pick-up, drop-off area to left of main lodge. Parking behind Slide In lodge.

OVERNIGHT ACCOMMODATIONS:

See the Alpental section, page 20.

BUSINESS ADDRESS:

Ski Lifts Inc.
7900 SE 28th Street Suite 200
Mercer Island, WA 98040
(206) 232-8182

STEVEN'S PASS AREA

5,800' top elevation   **1,800' vertical drop**

STEVEN'S PASS

Steven's Pass has had a gradual and well-orchestrated development over the years. The area attracts skiers from both the east and west sides of the Cascades.

There is a great diversity of runs, from gentle rolling slopes for intermediate and beginning skiers, to the steep mogul chutes of "Double Diamond, Solitude, and Rock Garden." The back side, Mill Valley, offers a choice of diamond runs to challenge the advanced and expert skier. Starting in the 1993-94 season, an additional "Jupiter" quad chairlift will move skiers up the mountain, giving them plenty of extra opportunities to take advantage of the variety of bowls and faces which make up this area.

Weekends in January, February and March bring a host of ski schools (about 20) in addition to the Steven's Pass Ski School. Lessons are available for all ages and abilities of enthusiasts. You can choose instruction in downhill skiing, snowboarding, telemark skiing, and big foot skiing.

There are also organized bus groups and charters who use the area regularly. There is a large readerboard at Monroe (west side of the Pass) which informs skiers of the area conditions. Consider planning your skiing trip around the daily schedule change, when skiers are arriving and departing. There are three optional ticket purchase times, 9 am, 12 noon, and 5 pm.

Just down the road is a recently developed Nordic Center. Called the "Cascade Depot," it emphasizes the Pacific Northern railroad history of this area. It is east of the main ski area about five miles and has about 25 kilometers (doubled since 1993 season) of groomed trails.

PHONE NUMBERS:
Information   (206) 973-2441
Snowline   (206) 634-1645
Ski School   (206) 973-2441

DIRECTIONS:

Steven's Pass is located at the summit on US Highway 2, east of Seattle. From Bothell, take Highway 522, then Highway 2 east at Monroe. From Everett travel east on Highway 2. From Leavenworth/Wenatchee, travel west on Highway 2.

DRIVING TIMES: (estimated)

Seattle	78 miles	1.5 hours
Wenatchee	58 miles	1 hour
Leavenworth	37 miles	40 minutes
Skykomish	16 miles	25 minutes
Everett	65 miles	1+ hour
Portland	258 miles	4.5 hours
Spokane	254 miles	4.5 hours
Boise	479 miles	9 hours

LIFT PRICES: (1993-94)

Monday and Tuesday All Ages $12
Wednesday to Friday All Ages $18
(Weekday tickets good from 9 am to 10 pm)
Sat/Sun/Holidays
Adult (13-61) $30
Child (7-12) $24
Senior (62-69) $26
Children 6 and under and Seniors over 70 ski *free*
Flexible ticketing program
Half-day on weekends at 12:00 pm

DAYS AND HOURS OF OPERATION:

Open daily   9:00 am to 10:00 pm
Night Skiing begins at 5:00 pm (ends in late March)
Spring Hours 9:00 am to 5:00 pm

STEVEN'S PASS INFORMATION AND FACILITIES:

RUNS	26
LIFTS	6 double chairs
	4 triple chairs
	3 rope tows
	1 quad

FOOD	West Lodge - deli and lounge
	T-Bar Lodge - T-Bar restaurant and lounge
	East Lodge - Express restaurant and lounge
	bakery and snack bar
AND MORE	Rental/repair - alpine and snowboard
	Ski Shop - accessories
	Ski Check - basket check
	Ski School
	RV parking in lot (self-contained)

SNOWBOARDING:
Lessons and rentals

CHILD CARE:
Weekends and holidays only in T-Bar Lodge
Reservations recommended **(206) 973-2441**
Toilet trained only (30 months to 6 years)

CROSS COUNTRY:
(Area is to the east of the ski area about 5 miles)
Daily trail pass:

Adults $6

Seniors and Children $5

Children 6 and under and seniors 70+ ski *free*
25+ km of trail
(New trails and improvements since the 1993 season)
Rental packages available
Open Friday to Sunday and holidays 9:00 am to 4:00 pm

SPECIAL INFORMATION:
READERBOARD: Driving from the west, pay attention to the readerboard at Monroe (on the left side of the highway) which tells the hours of operation, skiing conditions, and on rare occasions, the parking status.
ROAD: Do remember that you will be driving on a two-lane mountain pass and slides are possible during wet, heavy snow conditions. Driving from the east, Leavenworth and Wenatchee, beware of early icy road conditions through Tumwater Canyon.
DISABLED FACILITIES: There is an elevator and lavatories with wheelchair access in the West Lodge. Near the West Lodge is an unloading and parking zone.
EVENTS: HOT LINE from Everett **(206) 353-4400**

ENTERTAINMENT: There is frequently entertainment in Soft Landing lounge on weekends.

MINI MART: The Summit Mini Mart is open weekends (across highway from ski area) and has restrooms.

SKI SCHOOLS: Twenty plus Ski Schools operate at the area on weekends in addition to the resident ski school.

OVERNIGHT ACCOMMODATIONS:

LAKE WENATCHEE:

Lake Wenatchee Hideaways	1-509-763-2611
Squirrel Tree Inn	1-509-763-3157
Cougar Inn (north end of lake)	1-509-763-3354

LEAVENWORTH:

Evergreen Motor Inn	1-800-327-7212
Tyrolean Inn	1-509-548-5455
Bayern on the River	1-800-873-3960
Edelweiss Hotel	1-509-548-7015
Lodging House	1-800-253-8990
Der Ritterhof	1-509-548-5845
Obertal Motor Inn	1-800-537-9382
Enzian Motor Inn	1-800-223-8511
Bindlestiff's Riverside	1-509-763-3157
Village Inn	1-800-343-8198

DRYDEN: Junction of Highway 2 and Blewett Pass

Wedge Mountain Inn	1-509-548-6694

INDEX:

Bush House	1-206-793-2312

GOLDBAR:

Craig's Motel	1-206-793-1828

SULTAN:

Dutch Cup Motel	1-206-793-2215

SKYKOMISH:

Cascadia Hotel	1-206-677-2390
Hotel Skykomish	1-206-677-2477
Sky River Inn	1-206-677-2261

BUSINESS ADDRESS:

Steven's Pass Inc.
PO Box 98
Leavenworth, WA 98826
(206) 973-2441

Courtesy of Steven's Pass Inc.

WHITE PASS AREA

6,000' top elevation   **1,500' vertical drop**

WHITE PASS

You can cruise on the long two-mile run or have your choice of rolling cleared terrain, steep side chutes (with or without moguls), or groomed runs bordered by trees. There is a well-balanced variety of runs for beginner to expert. Additional areas are being considered for future development.

White Pass draws skiers from Yakima and the east side of the Cascades, as well as the Tacoma, Olympia and Seattle areas. The area gets an excellent snowfall (it is southeast of Mount Rainier) and has on-mountain condo accommodations at the Village Inn--complete with an outdoor heated swimming pool and restaurant. The ski area is just a walk across the highway! If you can't get reservations here, Packwood is a fun and affordable experience, and there are accommodations on the Yakima side of the pass also.

Across the road is White Pass Lake (frozen in the winter), which has a cross country ski trail surrounding it. A small grocery store/post office and gas station complete the resort area and provide the basic necessities for those who stay.

Steve and Phil Mahre (1984 Winter Olympic Gold and Silver medalists) lived, trained, and raced here, and continue to return to participate in special fund-raising events.

Winter Carnival in March and the annual Cowboy Bash are just two of the special events which are held here and can enhance your ski vacation. Live music is presented in the day lodge lounge several times during the season.

PHONE NUMBERS:
Information   (509) 453-8731
Snowline   (509) 672-3100

DIRECTIONS:
White Pass is at the summit of US Highway 12.
FROM SEATTLE, travel south on I-5 to Tacoma, exit onto Highway 127, then travel south on Highway 7 to Elbe, Morton and then Highway 12 to White Pass.
FROM PUYALLUP, travel south on Highway 161 to Elbe, then Highway 7 to Morton.
FROM YAKIMA, drive west on US 12.
FROM SOUTH OF CHEHALIS traveling north on I-5, exit on Highway 12 to Mossyrock/Yakima.

DRIVING TIMES: (estimated)

Seattle	190 miles	3.5 hours
Yakima	52 miles	1 hour
Packwood	20 miles	30 minutes
Portland	159 miles	3 hours
Randle	37 miles	40 minutes
Morton	55 miles	1 hour

LIFT PRICES: (1993-94)
WEEKENDS   Adults (13+) $26
                    Junior (6 to 12) $17
WEEKDAYS   Adults (M-T and F) $17
              Adults (Wed-Thur) $10
              Junior (all weekdays) $10
CHILDREN under 5 ski *free*
SENIOR (70+) ski *free*
Half-day tickets on sale 12:30 pm
Night skiing begins at 4:00 pm

DAYS AND HOURS OF OPERATION:
Open daily   8:45 am to 4:00 pm
Night skiing Friday and Saturday, Christmas Week and Holidays until 10:00 pm

WHITE PASS INFORMATION AND FACILITIES:
RUNS   14
LIFTS   4 double chairs
                 1 rope tow
                 1 poma

FOOD	Day lodge with cafeteria, and lounge
AND MORE	Rental/repair- alpine and nordic and
	snowboard
	Ski Shop - accessories
	Ski School (alpine and nordic)
	RV parking in lot across street from ski area
	(self-contained)

SNOWBOARDING:
Half-pipe
Snowboard rentals

CHILD CARE:
8:30 am to 4:30 pm
2 to 6 years
Day care includes a snack and lunch
Reservations recommended **1-509-672-3106**

CROSS COUNTRY:
Open daily
Trails groomed Thursday through Sunday
15 km of double track
Track pass $7

SPECIAL INFORMATION:
FACILITIES: There is a gas station, post office, and small grocery store within walking distance of the ski area and Village Inn.
ENTERTAINMENT: There is live music once a month in the day lodge lounge.
VILLAGE INN: There is a restaurant and heated outdoor swimming pool at the Village Inn. Inquire at Inn for usage.
SUMMER: Scenic chair rides are available from June to September , 9:00 am to 5:00 pm
CAYUSE PASS: In late spring, watch for the opening of Cayuse Pass (Highway 123). It is a convenient short-cut from Crystal Mountain to White Pass.

OVERNIGHT ACCOMMODATIONS:
WHITE PASS
Village Inn Condominiums	1-509-672-3131

PACKWOOD
Inn at Tatoosh Meadows	1-206-494-2311
Tatoosh Motel	1-206-494-5321
Cowlitz River Lodge	1-206-494-7338
Hotel Packwood	1-206-494-5431
Inn of Packwood	1-206-494-2191

MORTON
The Season's Motel	1-206-496-6835
Stiltner Motel	1-206-496-5103

EAST OF WHITE PASS
Silver Beach Resort	1-509-672-2499
Game Ridge Motel (Rimrock)	1-509-672-2212
Whistlin Jack Lodge	1-800-876-6696
(Nachese, Chinook Pass)	

BUSINESS ADDRESS:

White Pass Company, Inc.
PO Box 354
Yakima, WA 98907
(509) 453-8731

ADDITIONAL WASHINGTON SKI AREAS

These areas are smaller and operate on a varying schedule (usually only open on weekends or limited weekdays). They are sometimes run by organizations or groups local to the area. They lack the size and amenities of destination resorts, but can still provide a unique skiing experience. These areas are particularly enjoyable with young skiers or for families seeking a fun day of skiing without paying large lift fees. Each is definitely worth checking out. The phone numbers can change depending on the organization or person responsible for managing the area each year. In some cases, I have just listed the area code instead of a phone listing. Call information for a current listing.

BADGER MOUNTAIN (near Waterville)
(509)
Weekends only
Ski School
3 rope tows
Cross country trails
Sledding and snowmobile
Day lodge with cafeteria

ECHO VALLEY (near Lake Chelan)
1-800-4-CHELAN
Weekends and Wednesdays
3 rope tows
1 poma lift
Day lodge and coffee shop
Ski School
Ski rentals

HURRICANE RIDGE (near Port Angeles on the Olympic Peninsula)
(206) 457-5559
(206-452-0329 Road Report)
Weekends only
1 poma lift, 2 rope tows
Coffee shop and day lodge
Rentals
Ski School
Cross country trails

LEAVENWORTH SKI BOWL (near Leavenworth)
(509) 548-5115
2 rope tows
2 poma lifts
Day lodge
Rental and repair
Cross country

LOUP LOUP (near Omak)
(509) 826-2720 (recording)
2 poma lifts
1 rope tow
Day lodge
Ski rental
Ski Shop - accessories
Ski School
20K cross country track

SITZMARK (near Tonasket)
(509)
Weekends and mid-week
1 chair lift
1 rope tow
Day lodge and coffee shop
Ski rental
Ski School
Cross country

SQUILCHUCK SKI BOWL
(near Wenatchee on the way to Mission Ridge)
This area is operated by Wenatchee Valley College Ski Area
Management Program
(509) 662-1651
2 rope tows
Day lodge and coffee shop
5K cross country track
Sledding area
Ski School

Courtesy of the Armstrong Family.

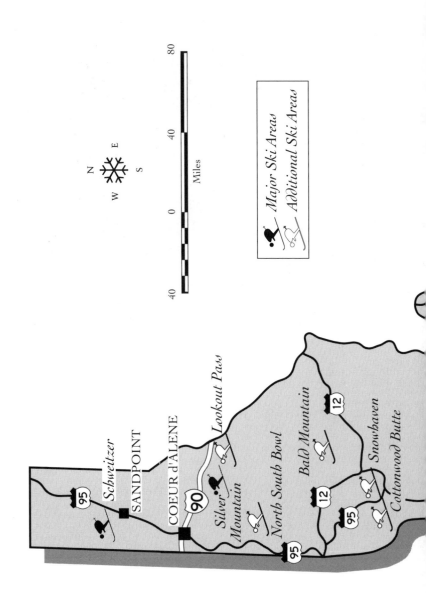

N
W E
S

80
40
0
40
Miles

Major Ski Areas
Additional Ski Areas

Schweitzer
SANDPOINT
95
COEUR d'ALENE
90
Silver Mountain
Lookout Pass
North South Bowl
Bald Mountain
12
12
Snowhaven
Cottonwood Butte
95
95

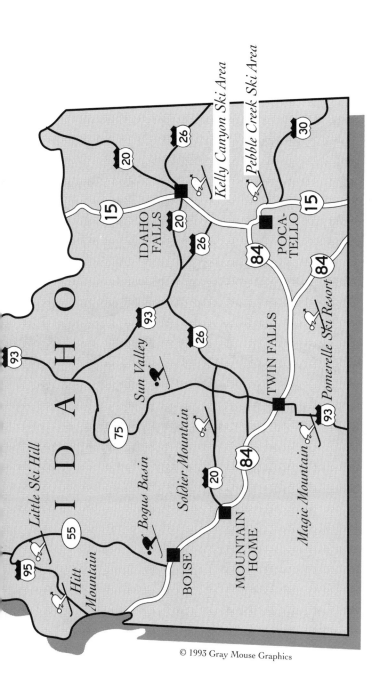

© 1993 Gray Mouse Graphics

BOGUS BASIN AREA

7,590' top elevation   **1,800' vertical drop**

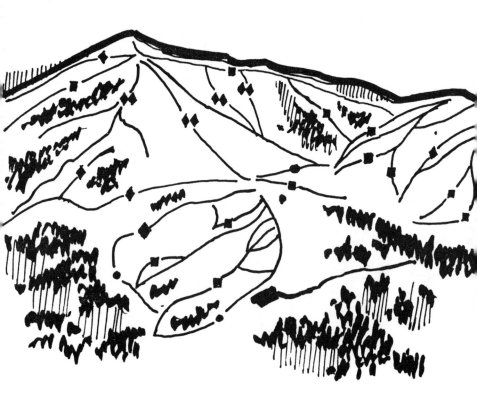

BOGUS BASIN

Bogus Basin can be found perched high above Boise at the top of a steep, winding, climbing, but well-maintained road. The views on the way up or down are spectacular. Several turn-out areas are provided for skiing photographers and slow drivers.

When you arrive in the area, you'll need to decide which lodge will be your day's destination. There are two day-lodges here separated by about two miles of road. The Bogus Creek Base Area is first, and if you need services such as rentals, lessons, or child care, this is where you will stop. The cross country area comes next on the road, and is between the two lodges. It has its own parking area and warming/ticketing hut.

At the end of the road is the upper lodge, Pioneer, which has a gift shop and eating facilities. Also nearby (walking distance) are the Pioneer Inn Condos which are the area's overnight accommodations. The condos are comfortable and are situated approximately in the center of the ski area. Besides the convenience of their location, all the units have a spectacular view.

The terrain is designed to accommodate all levels of skiing abilities, and offers a wide selection of runs. The design makes use of two mountains and their surrounding valleys. It is advisable to start with the easier runs and gain familiarity with the area, and also to orient your skiing to the chairlift destinations. For those who like ungroomed, "expert only runs," there are some very challenging areas. Also for those who like to ski the trees, there is an plenty of opportunity here.

The area celebrated its first 50 years in 1993. The discovery of gold here in the 1940's led to the discovery of the great skiing potential of this area. You will notice that all the mountain runs are named for gold mines.

PHONE NUMBERS:

Information	(208) 332-5401 (recording)
	(208) 332-5100 (mountain)
Statewide report	(800) 367-4397
Snowline	(208) 342-2100
Ski School	(208) 336-1234

DIRECTIONS:

Bogus Basin is located north of Boise, about 16 miles on Bogus Basin Road.

Driving on I-84 from the west, take the left lane, Exit 49 (Highway 184) towards the city center. Travel about 2.5 miles, then take the River Street Exit. Turn left onto 15th (a one-way street), then left on Hayes which becomes N. Harrison Blvd. After crossing Hill Road, turn right onto Bogus Basin Road. (There are prominent signs directing you to Bogus Basin from the River Street exit.) Once you leave the city of Boise, the road is a two-lane, maximum 25 mph, switchback road with lots of turn-outs for slow traffic. *Do not pass* , just appreciate the panoramic views!

DRIVING TIMES: (estimated)

Boise	16 miles	30 minutes
Spokane	438 miles	8.5 hours
Seattle (winter)	538 miles	9 hours
Portland	440 miles	7 hours

LIFT PRICES: (1993-94)

Adult (13-64) $25*
Senior (65+) $19*
Child (6-12) $17*
Pre First Grade Children ski *free*
Bitter Route Chair only $10 every day
Half-day begins at 1:00 pm
Night skiing begins at 4:00 pm
*Tickets must be purchased at Bogus Creek Area on weekdays.
  Pioneer Lodge is only open on weekends and holidays,
  from 9:00 am to 3:00 pm.
*Tickets are available at Pioneer Inn Condo's when the lodge is CLOSED.

DAYS AND HOURS OF OPERATION:

OPEN daily
Monday to Friday   9:00 am to 9:00 pm
Weekends and Holidays 9:00 am to 10:00 pm
Night skiing seven days a week

BOGUS BASIN INFORMATION AND FACILITIES:

RUNS   45
LIFTS   6 double chairs
            3 rope tows
FOOD   2 day lodges:
            Bogus Creek Lodge-cafe and bar
            Pioneer Lodge-cafe, saloon, and restaurant.
AND MORE   (all at Bogus Creek area)
            Rental/repair - alpine and snowboard
            Ski School *see Special information, on page 92*
            Ski Shop - accessories
            Gift Shop - souvenirs
            NASTAR

SNOWBOARDING:

Half-pipe
Rentals and lessons

CHILD CARE:

(located in the Bogus Creek Lodge)
6 months to 6 years
Monday to Thursday (days) Saturday and Sunday
Friday and Saturday nights until 10:00 pm
Certified day care
Reservations **(208) 336-4500**

CROSS COUNTRY:

(Nordic Center between lodges)
21 km of trail
Lessons and rentals available
Warming hut and waxing room
Operates 10:00 am to 4:00 pm
Trail passes:
Adults $5.00
Children $2.00
Cross country area is not patrolled mid-week.

SPECIAL INFORMATION:

COMMERCIAL TRANSPORTATION: Bogus Basin is very
convenient to Boise, which is served by major airlines, bus and
Amtrak.
BUS SERVICE: There is a local Bus service to the ski area on
weekends and holidays. Call **(208) 336-4500** for schedule

BUS SERVICE: Mid-week bus from Boise to Bogus from the Shaver's Food Store for all, ages 16 and older, or children accompanied by an adult **(208) 342-2100 or (800) 369-4511**.
SKI SCHOOL: The Ski School offers a wide variety of programs for every level and age of skiing as well as a special program for the physically challenged **(336-3293 or 344-6227)**.
CHILD CARE: Free child care is offered on Thursdays for those parents who are enrolled in the ski school program.
COLLEGE: Boise is home to Boise State University, and host to many sports activities and conventions. Accommodations can be limited. I advise advance reservations.
TIME CHANGE: If you are coming to Boise from Pacific Standard Time, you will gain one hour near Ontario, where you enter the Mountain Time zone.

OVERNIGHT ACCOMMODATIONS:
BOGUS BASIN

Pioneer Inn Condos	1-800-367-4397
(at the top of the ski area)	1-208-336-4500

BOISE

Holiday Inn	1-208-344-8365
Best Western Safari	1-208-344-6556
Littletree Inn	1-208-343-7505
Rodeway Inn	1-208-376-2700
University Inn	1-208-345-7170
Nendels Inn	1-208-344-4030
Shilo Inn -Riverside	1-208-433-3521
Red Lion Motor Inn (Downtowner)	1-208-344-7691
Comfort Inn	1-800-228-5150
Statehouse Inn	1-208-342-4622
Super 8	1-208-344-8871

For additional accommodations call the:
Boise Entertainment and Event Host Line
                                                1-800-342-HOST
Convention and Visitors Bureau   1-800-635-5240

BUSINESS ADDRESS:
Bogus Basin
2405 Bogus Basin Road
Boise, ID 82702
(208) 332-5151

Courtesy of Bogus Basin. Photo by Mary Davis.

BRUNDAGE MOUNTAIN AREA

7,640' top elevation   **1,800' vertical drop**

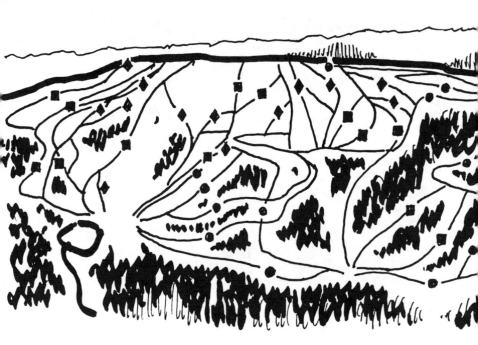

BRUNDAGE MOUNTAIN

This ski area, just a short drive from McCall, is being "discovered" by more skiers each year who are in search of a less expensive vacation, good skiing terrain, and a unique small town experience.

McCall is a summer and winter resort town and offers a nice variety of overnight accommodations, interesting activities and special events. (The surrounding area also seems to be on the threshold of major resort development.)

Most well-known of the area's annual events is the Winter Carnival, which takes place each year at the end of January, and runs for a week into February. There are a torchlight parade, humorous competitions (like an outhouse race on the frozen lake!), dances, bingo, a snowflake ball, ski movies, theatrics, ice skating, and the most exceptional snow sculpturing contest with displays all over the town created by local and state teams.

At Brundage, you'll find 36 clearly defined runs cut through the tree-covered slopes. You'll also discover runs which fall from the ridge above the ski lodge, spread into the two valleys, and flow down multiple side hills. There is a nice balance of easy to intermediate to difficult runs, which makes the area fun for multi-level groups and families. The snow is usually powder here, and the area groomers keep it nicely packed. Once you get to the top of the mountain, the view is of Payette Lakes, mountains and more mountains.

PHONE NUMBERS:
Information   (208) 634-7462
Snowline   (208) 634-5650

DIRECTIONS:

Brundage Mountain is only nine miles from downtown McCall.
McCall is reached by driving north of Boise on Highway 55.
Scenic Highway 55 begins in Boise off State Street at the 'Lil
Stinker Gas Station.
From Lewiston drive south on Highway 95, at New Meadows
continue south on Highway 55.
Driving east on I-84, exit at Fruitland/Payette and drive to
New Meadows on Highway 55 or take Exit 46 to McCall/Eagle
just before reaching Boise. (For the best winter driving
conditions, I would use I-84 and Highway 55 from Boise.)
The Highways from all directions are very scenic and mostly
two-lane.

DRIVING TIMES: (estimated)

Seattle(via Boise)	630 miles	10 hours
Seattle(via Lewiston)	550 miles	10 hours
Boise	108 miles	2 hours
Portland	460 miles	8+ hours
Spokane	269 miles	5 hours
Lewiston	169 miles	2.5 hours
Fruitland	99 miles	2 hours
McCall	9 miles	12 minutes

LIFT PRICES: (1993-94)

Adult (13-64) $23
Child (6 -13) $16
Seniors (65+) $18
Children under 5 ski *free*
Half-day begins at 1:00 pm

DAYS AND HOURS OF OPERATION:

Monday to Friday   10:00 am to 4:00 pm
Saturday/Sunday and holidays 9:00 am to 4:00 pm
Open daily
NO NIGHT SKIING

BRUNDAGE INFORMATION AND FACILITIES:

RUNS	36
LIFTS	1 triple chair
	2 double chairs
	2 rope tows
	1 platter pull
	(separate lift pass to use platter pull only)
FOOD	Day lodge with cafeteria
AND MORE	Ski School
	Ski Shop - accessories
	Rental/repair-alpine and snowboard and telemark
	RV parking in lot - self contained
	(more RV accommodations in McCall)
	Lockers in lodge

SNOWBOARDING:

Half-pipe
Snowboard rentals

CHILD CARE: (The Bunny Hutch)

State Licensed
Located in the main lodge
Open daily
6 weeks to 8 years
Reservations **(208) 634-7462**

SPECIAL INFORMATION:

AIRPORT: McCall has a small airport for use by private aircraft. It is also an easy commute from Boise, which has full travel service with Amtrak, bus line, and a commercial airport.

RESORT: McCall is on the shores of Payette Lake and has summer and winter activities.

EVENTS: January is the "Winter Carnival" which includes a torchlight parade, contests, dances, games and fantastic snow sculptures displayed throughout the town! If you plan on traveling here during this festival, *get reservations early.*

HOT SPRINGS: Zim's Hot Springs is four miles north of New Meadows and has a swimming and hot soaking pool, recreation hall and snack bar. A fun diversion after a day on the slopes!

SNOWMOBILING: The area around McCall has excellent terrain for snowmobiling and cross country skiing.
TIME ZONE: McCall is in the Mountain Time zone. Driving north the time changes back to Pacific Time at Riggens.

OVERNIGHT ACCOMMODATIONS:
McCALL

Mill Park Condos	1-208-634-4151 or
	1-800-888-7544
Scandia Inn Motel	1-208-634-7394
Hotel McCall	1-208-634-8105
Riverside Motel and Condos	1-208-634-5610
Shore Lodge	1-208-634-2244
Village Inn Motel	1-208-634-2344
Woodsman Motel	1-208-634-7671
Brundage Bungalows	1-208-634-8573

CONDO RENTALS

Engen Real Estate	1-208-634-2114
McCall Vacations	1-208-634-7056
Clark Property Rentals	1-208-634-7766
Johnson and Co Condominiums	1-208-634-7134

BUSINESS ADDRESS:
Brundage Mountain Company
Box 1062
McCall, ID 83638
(208)634-4151 or
(800)888-7544

Courtesy of Brundage Mountain Company.
Photo by Scott Spiker.

SCHWEITZER MOUNTAIN AREA

6,389' top elevation (Schweitzer side) **2,400' vertical drop**
6,400' top elevation (Colburn side) **2,400' vertical drop**

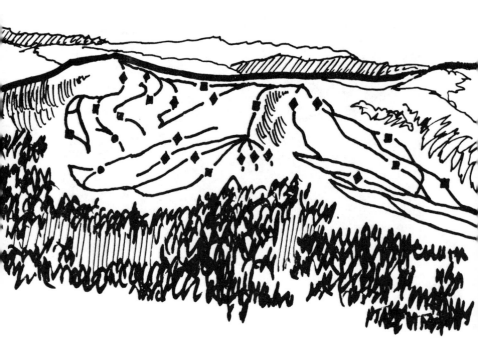

SCHWEITZER MOUNTAIN

Schweitzer is well underway to completing a ten-year expansion which culminates in the year 2000. The goal is to build a destination resort on the mountain with ski in-and-out accommodations, private homes and condos, and to develop more lifts and trails. Many improvements have occurred in the last few years.

An entire village is evolving which now contains an elegant hotel, restaurant and lounge. Skier services for rental and repair have been grouped together for accessibility and convenience. The best news (for those who have not been here recently) is that the road to the mountain has been widened, paved, and improved.

The Headquarters Day Lodge has four levels of skier services for all ages of travelers. Its design has been honored by *Snow Country* magazine (look on the stairs for the display of the magazine lay-out). Attached to the lodge is an enormous sun-deck for eating or sunning. A large ski check area for day or night storage is underneath.

For those who like long runs, there is a wide selection on the Colburn side of the mountain-some containing chutes and moguls. On the Schweitzer side, there is a very accessible bowl to ski and some serious double diamond runs off the ridge. The majority of the runs are about 50% intermediate and 25% advanced. The other 25% of runs are for beginner skiers. These runs are in more open terrain and closer to the lodge. The variety of skiing terrain combined with the number of runs is enough to keep you exploring all day long.

If you don't stay on the mountain, the town of Sandpoint (which is a summer resort town) is at the base. Sandpoint sits on the shores of Lake Pend Oreille and has many accommodations and activities to keep you busy in the after-ski hours. Schweitzer is also a comfortable drive from Coeur d'Alene.

PHONE NUMBERS:

Information	**(208) 263-9555**
Snowline	**(208) 263-9562**
Ski School	**(208) 263-9555**

DIRECTIONS:

Schweitzer is in the Selkirk mountains about 11 miles from Sandpoint, Idaho and about 75 miles from Spokane, Washington.
Driving east or west on I-90, exit at Coeur d'Alene north on Highway 95 to Hayden and Sandpoint. You will drive through the town of Sandpoint and then exit left to the ski area, at the prominent signs.

DRIVING TIMES: (estimated)

Coeur d'Alene	55 miles	1+ hour
Spokane		
(1-90 and Highway 55)	75 miles	1.5 hours
Spokane		
(Highway 395 and 2)	95 miles	2 hours
Sandpoint	11 miles	25 minutes
Seattle	352 miles	6 hours
Portland	457 miles	8 hours
Boise(two-lane road)	448 miles	8+ hours

LIFT PRICES: (1993-94)

Adult (18-64) $32
Student (7-17) $25
(Student can be full time college student, bring your ID)
Senior (65+) $23
Children under 6 ski *free*
Half-day skiing begins at 12:30 pm
Night skiing begins at 4:00 pm

DAYS AND HOURS OF OPERATION:

Open daily   9:00 am to 4:00 pm
Night skiing Thursday, Friday, Saturday
and Holidays until 10:00 pm

SCHWEITZER INFORMATION AND FACILITIES:

RUNS	48
LIFTS	5 double chairs
	1 high speed detachable quad
FOOD	Headquarters day lodge:
	Cafeteria, 2 restaurants, deli, 3 lounges
	On mountain cafeteria - Outback Inn

AND MORE   Ski School
3 Ski Shops - ski apparel and accessories,
   gifts, and souvenir items
Rental/repair- alpine, cross country,
   telemark, and snowboard
Video "Game Area" in lodge
NASTAR racing - weekends and holidays
Computerized race course:
   Wednesday to Friday 50¢
Snowmaking

SNOWBOARDING:
Half-pipe
Snowboard rentals

CHILD CARE: (Kinder Camp)
2 months to 12 years
8:30 am to 4:30 pm
Reservations: (208) 263-9555

CHURCH SERVICES:
Schweitzer Chapel
Catholic Mass, Saturday at 4:30 pm
Protestant Service, Sunday at 11:30 am

CROSS COUNTRY:
8 km of *free* trails

SPECIAL INFORMATION:
SANDPOINT: Sandpoint is located on the shores of Lake Pend
Oreille (pronounced "pond o-ray") and is also a summer resort
town. There are an excellent variety of shops, services and
restaurants.
TRANSPORTATION: Sandpoint is serviced by Amtrak, and
Spokane (75 miles away) has a commercial airport.
Sandpoint has a small airport for private and corporate
aircraft.
MOVIES: *Free* movies for children in the Headquarters Day
Lodge on Saturday nights.

LIFT TICKET: *Skier Guarantee Lift ticket-* if snow conditions do not meet your expectations, you may return your ticket (within one hour of purchasing) for a voucher for another day.
CHILDREN: Parents with young children should inquire about the ski and stay *free* program. This area really caters to economical family skiing.
ROAD: The road up to the ski area has been re-surfaced, but does have some sharp switch-back turns. Maximum speed is 30 mph.
VAN SERVICE: Some motels offer van service to and from the mountain; ask when making reservations.
ROAD: Highway 2 from Spokane to Newport to Sandpoint is a two-lane road which I do not recommend for winter travel. It is in poor condition and traveled by large trucks which have difficulty negotiating the narrow road and delay traffic. Take I-90 to Coeur d'Alene and Highway 95 to Sandpoint for easier, relaxed driving.

OVERNIGHT ACCOMMODATIONS:
SCHWEITZER MOUNTAIN

Green Gables Lodge	1-208-265-0257
Overniter Lodge	1-208-263-9564
Condos (Central Reservations)	1-800-831-8810

SANDPOINT

Connie's Best Western	1-208-263-9581
The Lakeside	1-800-543-8126
The Edgewater	1-800-635-2534
Best Spa Motel	1-208-263-3532
Super 8	1-800-843-1991 or
	1-208-263-2210
Monarch Inn	1-800-543-8193
K2 Motel	1-208-263-3441
S and W Motel	1-208-263-5979
Quality Inn	1-208-263-2111

BUSINESS ADDRESS:
Schweitzer, Inc.
PO Box 815
Sandpoint, Idaho 83864
(208) 263-9555

SILVER MOUNTAIN AREA

6,300' top elevation   **2,200' vertical drop**

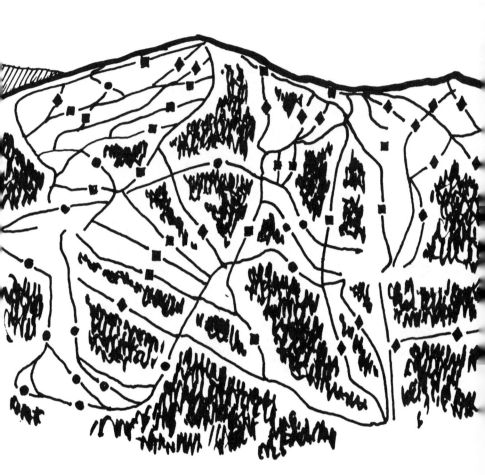

SILVER MOUNTAIN

Silver Mountain entered the ski scene in 1991 as the newest of developing destination ski areas. Lots of "hoopla" surrounded the opening, and the area strives to live up to the advertisements. The history of the resurrection of this area is worthy of comment. It is owned by the town of Kellogg. Local leaders believed that the ski area could help rebuild their economy, which had fallen with the price of silver. They knew that the skiing and snow on the mountain were great, but a winding, switchback road discouraged many skiers and development. Enter one man's vision of a gondola up the mountainside, and you have the short version of the transformation of the former Jackass Ski Bowl and Silverhorn ski areas.

Skier services are strongly emphasized at this area. The feeling from the moment you get on the gondola (don't forget to buy your coffee and roll) is one of relaxation and luxury. There is even a *Gondola Gazette*, which provides interesting area information for you to read as you rise above the valley floor.

The base area has an unloading zone and valet parking if you wish. When disembarking at Mountain Haus (the mid-mountain lodge) take some time to explore this facility before you out on the mountain. It holds a treasure of eating areas, from a cafeteria to the Alpenrose restaurant (make reservations to eat here), and services. The child care center is located on the lower level. All service areas are staffed with exceptionally friendly people to answer your questions. Outside is a *free* ski check area where your skis can receive a complimentary waxing.

The skiing terrain is a mixture of groomed intermediate runs and mogul side hills on the Kellogg Peak side. On the farther Wardner side are the more challenging black diamond runs, which include tree and chute skiing and steeper pitches. Intermediate skiers have their choice of runs such as "Gold, Tamarack, Sunrise and Northstar," plus the longest run, "Centennial." Beginners have a nice area below Mountain Haus on the wide and well-groomed runs of "Ross and Noah."

There are convenient accommodations in the town of Kellog. However, if you need after-ski activities and shopping malls, plan to stay in Coeur d'Alene.

PHONE NUMBERS:

Information	(208) 783-1111
Snowline	(208) 783-1111
From Spokane	(509) 747-0221
Ski School	(208) 783-1111

DIRECTIONS:

Silver Mountain is off Interstate I-90 in Kellog, Idaho. Take exit 49 (Bunker Avenue) and drive a quarter mile to the large parking lot. Then take a relaxing 19-minute Gondola ride to the mountain.

DRIVING TIMES: (estimated)

Kellogg	0 miles, Silver Mountain is a gondola ride away!	
Wallace	10 miles	15 minutes
Coeur d'Alene	35 miles	35 minutes
Spokane	66 miles	1+ hour
Boise	411 miles	7.5 hours
Seattle	345 miles	6+ hours
Portland	454 miles	8+ hours

LIFT PRICES: (1993-94)

Adult (18-64) $31
Senior (65+) $24
Junior (13-17) $24
College (ID required - full time student) $24
Child (7-12) $18
Children 6 and under ski *free*
Half-day (late arrivals) begins at 12:30

DAYS AND HOURS OF OPERATION:

Lifts open daily 9:00 am to 3:15 and 4:00 pm

GONDOLA OPERATION:

Gondola opens Monday to Friday at 8:30 am
Gondola closes Monday to Thursday at 5:00 pm
Gondola opens Saturday and Sunday at 8:00 am
Gondola closes Saturday and Sunday at 6:00 pm
Night skiing Friday evenings until 10:00 pm
Gondola closes about 10:00 pm on Friday

SILVER MOUNTAIN INFORMATION AND FACILITIES:

RUNS   50
LIFTS   Gondola to mid-mountain (19-minute ride)
                1 quad chair
                2 triple chairs
                2 double chair
                1 handle pull
FOOD   Base Village - gondola, restaurant and bar
                  and cafe
                Mountain Haus Lodge - restaurant,
                  cafeteria, deli, lounge
                Alpenrose Restaurant, (upper lodge level)
                Reservations **208-783-1111** ext 307
                Tamarack Lodge (original lodge) cafeteria
AND MORE   **BASE AREA:**
                Rental/repair (alpine and telemark) Loulou's
                Two gift-souvenir shops
                Timbers restaurant
                MOUNTAIN HAUS:
                Ski School
                Rental/repair (snowboards) Loulou's
                  (call to reserve snowboards)
                Accessories for snowboards
                Recreational racing program - weekends
                  and holidays
                Snowmaking

SNOWBOARDING:

Two half-pipes (natural and man-made)
Special area on mountain reserved *just* for snowboarders!
Rentals and lessons

CHILD CARE: (Minor's Camp)

Located in Mountain Haus
Children ages 2 to 6
State licensed day care
Reservations **(208) 783-1111**
(Telephones located in both lodges will connect you to Minor's
Camp)

SPECIAL INFORMATION:

SKI CHECK: Complimentary ski check and waxing while you eat lunch or breakfast or just take a break.

GONDOLA: Remember that you *must* ride the gondola down at the end of the day, so plan accordingly. If the lines are long, ski another run or go inside the Mountain Haus and enjoy the services and entertainment on the weekends. Chair #1 runs the longest (until 4:00 pm).

COFFEE: If you get your coffee cup marked as you purchase your first cup, and then save your cup, you can get *free* refills all day.

ENTERTAINMENT: Timbers, a restaurant at the base, also offers weekend entertainment.

BAG CHECK AND SKI STORAGE: You can check your bag of ski goodies or use the changing room in Mountain Haus. If you are skiing multiple days, you can get overnight ski and boot storage at Mountain Haus.

VALET SERVICE: There is valet service (weekends only) at the base; they guarantee a warm car (for a fee) waiting for you at the end of the day.

COMMERCIAL TRANSPORTATION: Commercial air service, Amtrak and bus line service at Coeur d'Alene or Spokane.

RENTAL ACCOMMODATIONS: Many houses in the Kellogg and Wallace are rented as condos and chalets. You can request a brochure from the area which has pictures of the accommodations so you will know what you are renting.

SKI PACKAGES: Most motels offer a ski package, and some even offer limo or bus service to and from the mountain. Local business sponsors offer discount coupons for tickets. It is worth checking into when you arrive.

SKI RENTALS: If you are going to rent skis, do it at the Gondola Base in Loulou's.

SNOWBOARD RENTALS: If you are going to rent a snowboard, go up to Loulou's in the Mountain Haus.

OVERNIGHT ACCOMMODATIONS:
KELLOGG

Silverhorn Motor Inn	1-800-437-6437 or
	1-208-783-1151
Trail Motel	1-208-784-1161
Sunshine Inn	1-208-784-1186
Kellog International Hostel	1-208-783-4171
Silver Mountain Prpty Mgmt	1-800-621-2963
Super 8 (opening November 1993)	1-800-785-5443

WALLACE

Best Western Wallace Inn	1-208-782-1252
Stardust Motel	1-208-752-1252
Historic Jameson Hotel	1-208-752-1252

COEUR D'ALENE

Coeur d'Alene Resort	1-800-688-5253 or
	1-208-765-4000
Day's Inn	1-208-667-8668
Flamingo Motel	1-208-664-2159
Comfort Inn	1-208-765-5300
Coeur d'Alene Holiday Inn	1-208-765-3200
Pines Resort Motel	1-208-664-8244
Super 8 Motel	1-208-765-8880
Shilo Inn	1-800-222-2244
Silver Lake Motel	1-208-772-8595
Red Rose Motel	1-208-664-3167
Sundowner Motel	1-208-667-9787

BUSINESS ADDRESS:
Silver Mountain
610 Bunker Avenue
Kellogg, ID 83837
(208) 783-1111

Courtesy of Silver Mountain.

BALD MOUNTAIN AREA
(SUN VALLEY)

9,150' top elevation   **3,400' vertical drop**

RIVER RUN

SUN VALLEY

Sun Valley is perhaps the most well-known of the destination ski areas in the three states. It has been a destination ski area since 1936, and is a year-round resort area with almost as many people visiting in the summer as in the winter. It is a world class resort and continues to meet the expectations of all who come here.

Many accommodation choices are available. You can stay in the Sun Valley Village area, in the lodge or surrounding condos, in the Elkhorn/Raddison area, in one of many motel choices in Ketchum, or at the bottom of the mountain in the Warm Springs area.

There are plenty of amenities available to fill after-skiing hours: ice skating, cross country centers and trails, horse-drawn sleigh rides, snowmobiling, movies, entertainment, a wide variety of stores and boutiques. There are more than enough eating choices to suit every taste and pocketbook.

An extra convenience in the area is the connecting *free* bus system (KART) which runs all over the valley and can take you to and from the slopes as well as to dinner, etc. It makes travel in the area *free* of car use and gives pre-teen and older children a wonderful sense of independence.

On the mountain, there are snowmaking machines practically everywhere, which guarantee snow from November 25th to May 1st. There are two on-mountain lodges and a beautifully designed base lodge at Warm Springs. New facilities are under construction at the base of River Run and at the top of Seattle Ridge. All the runs are well-groomed and designed to delight the intermediate to expert skier. The Ski school meets at the top of the mountain, and rental equipment is available from area stores.

If you are a beginner skier, go to Dollar Mountain (closer to Sun Valley). Lessons are available here for every age skier. The terrain is excellent for building confidence, and expert ski instructors cater to your all special needs.

PHONE NUMBERS:

Information	**1-800-635-8261 or**
	1-208-622-4111
Snowline	**1-800-635-4150 or**
	1-208-622-4111
Ski School	**1-208-622-2248**
Sun Valley Sports Center	**1-208-622-2231**

DIRECTIONS:

The resort of Sun Valley is just north of the town of Ketchum, which is north of Twin Falls on Highway 93. Coming from the east or west on I-84, exit at Twin Falls north on Highway 93. At Shoshone, continue north on Highway 75 to Bellevue, Hailey and Ketchum. Turn right at the major intersection in downtown Ketchum and drive three quarter miles to Sun Valley resort.

From the east on I-84 you can exit at Mountain Home, taking Highway 20 to Fairfield and then at the intersection of Highways 75 and 20, go north on Highway 75 a short twenty-seven miles to Ketchum. However, I advise you to inquire about winter road conditions before you take this short-cut. It can have extreme winter conditions, i.e. snow drifts, ice, etc., that make it hazardous.

From the west, take Highway 26 from Bliss to Shoshone which saves a little time if Highway 20 is questionable.

From Idaho Falls, take Highway 20 to Arco and Carey. This route connects to Highway 75 approximately 20 miles west of Carey. This road can also have extreme winter conditions.

DRIVING TIMES: (estimated)

Twin Falls	83 miles	1.5 hours
Boise*	154 miles	2.5+ hours
Seattle*	687 miles	11-12 hours
Spokane	586 miles	10+ hours
Portland*	625 miles	10+ hours

*mostly Interstate freeway driving

LIFT PRICES: (1993-94)
BALDY MOUNTAIN LIFTS
(advanced skiing)
Adult (12+) $45
Child (11 and under) $25
Half-day begins at 1:00 pm
Multiple day lift passes may be purchased at a savings
Senior rates are available for those 65+

DOLLAR MOUNTAIN LIFTS (1993-94)
(beginning skiing)
Adult $24
Child $17

DOLLAR MOUNTAIN AREA
(SUN VALLEY)

6,638' top elevation

628' vertical drop

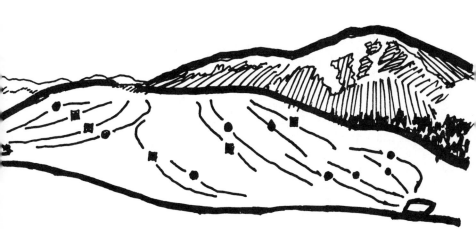

DAYS AND HOURS OF OPERATION:
(Both Baldy and Dollar Mountains)
Daily operation 9:00 am to 4:00 pm
No night skiing

SUN VALLEY INFORMATION AND FACILITIES:
This area is somewhat different from most in that the resort of
Sun Valley is a short distance from the major ski area, Bald
Mountain. The town of Ketchum spreads between them and the
resort of Elkhorn-Radisson is a stone's throw to the east.
Whereas most ski areas are central to their lodge and its
facilities, the lodges on Bald Mountain mainly serve as eating,
comfort, resting, ski school meeting areas and ticketing places.
Services such as ski rentals, etc., are available at business in
the resorts of Sun Valley and Elkhorn, or from ski businesses in
Ketchum and at the Warm Springs base of Baldy.
Sun Valley has two separate ski areas. Skiing nearest the
resort is at a smaller area (Dollar Mountain), with excellent
beginning and intermediate terrain for children and adults.

DOLLAR MOUNTAIN
(Half Dollar Mountain and Quarter Dollar Mountain)

RUNS	13
LIFTS	4
FOOD	Dollar Cabin Lodge-cafeteria
AND MORE	Snowmaking
	Ski School

BALD MOUNTAIN (Baldy)
(For advanced intermediate to expert skiers)

RUNS	60
LIFTS	2 double chairs
	5 triple chairs
	4 quads
FOOD	Base Lodge at Warm Springs
	Round House - mid mountain
	Lookout Lodge-restaurant at summit
	Seattle Ridge Lodge -(under construction)
	River Run Lodge -(under construction)
AND MORE	Sun Valley Ski School meets at Lookout
	Lodge/restaurant
	Snowmaking
	NASTAR (Warm Springs)

SNOWBOARDING:

No half-pipe, no special facilities.
Rentals at local stores.

SPECIAL INFORMATION:

KART: (Ketchum Area Rapid Transit **208-726-7140**) connects the resorts, the ski areas and streets of Ketchum. It is a *free* bus service for everyone. All buses are equipped with ski storage on the outside. The KART buses run from 7:30 am to 12 midnight (Red Route) and 9:00 am to 8:00 pm (Blue Route), about every 15 to 20 minutes from marked locations.

BASE AREAS: There are **two** base areas on Bald Mountain. One is at **Warm Springs** (about two miles from Ketchum) and the other is at **River Run** (at the south end of Ketchum).

WARM SPRINGS: A spectacular new base lodge was built here in 1992. There are also several gift and ski stores, rental and repair for ski, boots and snowboards, eating places, entertainment, and condo rentals in this area. Unless you are staying there, there is very limited parking at Warm Springs. Use the *free* KART bus (Red Bus Route) from the park and ride lot on Warm Springs Road or from designated bus pick-up areas throughout the valley.

RIVER RUN: It is closer to downtown Ketchum, at the southwest corner. Coming from Hailey, make a left turn just after the big white barn and just before the Lift Tower Lodge. There is a parking lot here, and it is also served by the *free* KART bus, but it is on the Blue Bus Run.

SUN VALLEY BUSES: Sun Valley Company also operates *free* ski buses for their guests and the public between Sun Valley, Ketchum, and Baldy and Dollar Mountains.

AIRLINES: Several commercial airlines fly to the Boise, Hailey, and Twin Falls airports. Connecting buses are scheduled from Boise and Twin Falls and shuttles are available from the Hailey airport.

BUS: Connecting bus rides are regularly scheduled during the winter season and are available from the Boise airport to Sun Valley.

ENTERTAINMENT: Sleigh rides, ice skating, a movie theater, bowling and ice hockey games are available in the area.

LIFT TICKETS: Discount tickets are available for "pre-season," skiing from the Sun Valley Sports Center. Also full-time college students be sure to carry college ID and inquire about discount tickets. Lift ticket packages for multiple days of skiing are available at a savings as well. There are also some

"special weeks" of bargain skiing here during January.
CHILDREN: There are some "kids stay and ski *free*" packages
at the Sun Valley Company hotel and condominiums and other
participating condo and hotels. Inquire when calling for dates
and requirements when making reservations.

CROSS COUNTRY SKIING:
Sun Valley Nordic Center
70 km of trails
Also cross country skiing is available at Elkhorn Nordic, Warm
Springs Nordic Center, and the Idaho Rocky Mountain Ranch.
Non-commercial trails ($ donations requested for use) are at
Redfish Lake, Alturas Lake, Galena, Prarie Creek,
North Fork, Lake Creek, and Wood River.

CHILD CARE:
Children's Playschool (Sun Valley Mall)
(208) 622-4111 ext. 2288
Child's Place **(208) 726-3240**
Elkhorn Children's Center **(800) 622-4101** or **(208) 622-4104**
Also check the local telephone directory.

OVERNIGHT ACCOMMODATIONS:
SUN VALLEY
CENTRAL LODGING/CONDOMINIUMS
                                    1-800-634-3347

SUN VALLEY
Sun Valley Inn   1-800-622-4111
Sun Valley Lodge   1-800-786-8259

ELKHORN
Raddison/Elkhorn Resort   1-800-ELK-HORN or
                                    1-208-622-4511

KETCHUM
River Street Inn   1-208-726-3611
Heidelberg Inn   1-208-726-5361
Best Western Tyrolean Lodge   1-208-726-5336
Warm Springs Property Mngmt   1-800-635-4404
River Run Lodge   1-208-726-9086

Best Western Christiania Lodge	1-800-535-3241
Christophe Condo and Hotel	1-208-726-5601
Boulder Mountain Hotel	1-208-726-5900
Bald Mountain Lodge	1-800-892-7407
Lift Tower Lodge	1-800-462-8646
Knob Hill Inn	1-208-726-8010

(These are just a few of the accommodations available. Check with a travel agent for more lodging and special ski packages offered by airlines, resorts and hotels.)

BUSINESS ADDRESS:
The Sun Valley Company
Sun Valley, ID 83353
(208) 622-4111

Courtesy of The Sun Valley Company.
Sleigh Ride to Trail Creek.

ADDITIONAL IDAHO SKI AREAS

These areas are smaller and operate on a varying schedule (usually open only on weekends or limited weekdays). They are sometimes run by organizations or groups local to the area. They lack the size and amenities of destination resorts, but can still provide a unique skiing experience. These areas are particularly enjoyable with young skiers or for families seeking a fun day of skiing without paying large lift fees. Each is definitely worth checking out. The phone numbers can change depending on the organization or person responsible for managing the area each year. In some cases, I have just listed the area code instead of a phone listing. Call information for a current listing.

BALD MOUNTAIN (near Pierce)
(208)
1 rope tow
1 T-bar
Day lodge/snack bar
Rentals

COTTONWOOD BUTTE (near Cottonwood)
(208)
1 rope tow
1 T-bar
Day lodge/snack bar

HITT MOUNTAIN (near Midvale)
(208)
1 rope tow
1 T-bar
Day lodge with cafeteria

KELLY CANYON SKI AREA (near Idaho Falls)
1-208-538-6261
3 double chairlifts
Rental/repair
Day lodge with cafeteria

LITTLE SKI HILL (near McCall)
1-208-634-5691
Alpine and nordic
1 T-bar
Ski School and race programs
Day lodge with cafeteria

LOOKOUT PASS (near Wallace, on border of Montana)
1-208-744-1301
1 double chair
Day lodge with cafeteria and bar
1 rope tow
Rental/repair
Ski shop - accessories

MAGIC MOUNTAIN (near Albion and Twin Falls)
1-208-735-2527
2 double chairlifts
1 rope tow
1 platter pull
Day lodge with cafeteria
Rentals

NORTH SOUTH BOWL (near Emida and Moscow on
Highway 95A)
(208)
1 rope tow
Rentals
Day lodge with cafeteria

POMERELLE SKI RESORT (near Albion)
1-208-638-5599
2 chairlifts
1 rope tow
Rental/repair
Ski School
Day lodge with cafeteria

PEBBLE CREEK SKI AREA (near Pocatello)
1-208-775-4451
3 chairlifts
Day Lodge with restaurant and lounge
Rentals
Ski School

SNOWHAVEN (near Grangeville)
(208)
1 rope tow
1 T-bar
Ski School
Snack bar
Ski Shop - accessories

SOLDIER MOUNTAIN (near Fairfield)
1-208-764-2260
2 chair lifts
1 rope tow
Snack bar
Ski School

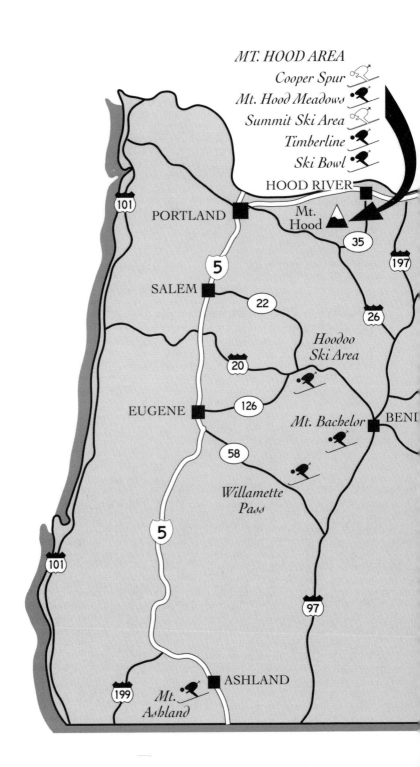

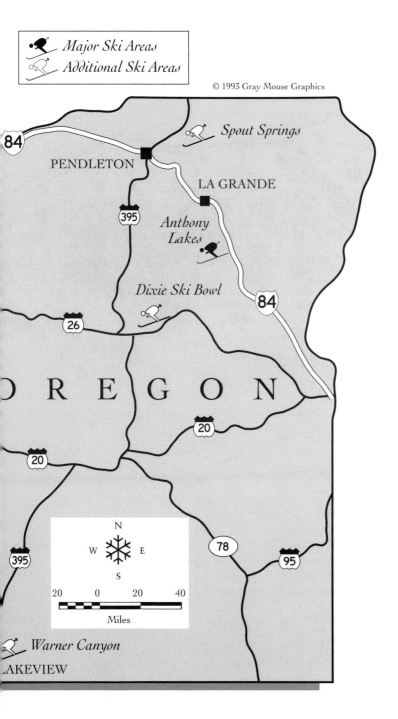

Major Ski Areas
Additional Ski Areas

© 1993 Gray Mouse Graphics

84

Spout Springs

PENDLETON

LA GRANDE

395

*Anthony
Lakes*

Dixie Ski Bowl

84

26

O R E G O N

20

20

N
W E
S

395

78

95

20   0   20   40

Miles

Warner Canyon

LAKEVIEW

ANTHONY LAKES AREA

8,000' top elevation   **900' vertical drop**

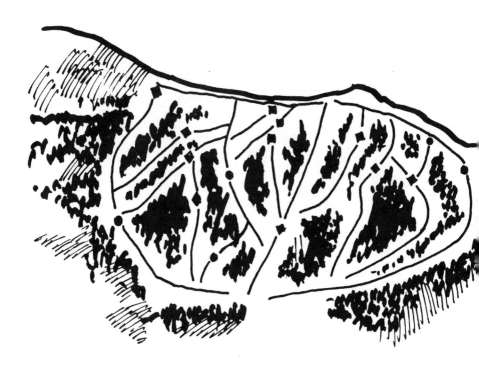

ANTHONY LAKES

This small ski area, which is a little off the beaten track, has a charming, small town feeling. The staff and skiers are exceptionally friendly and dedicated to providing a fun day of skiing on outstanding terrain.

Located off the I-84 Highway, it is accessible to skiers from Pendleton to Ontario, Oregon. However, you will find skiers who come here from as far as Walla Walla, Portland and even Boise.

La Grande is the home of Eastern Oregon State College, so you will find college students skiing and practicing their racing skills here along with the community families. Ski tour buses also find their way up to the ski area during the season.

However, the majority of the skiers are locals with interesting stories to tell about the development of the area and its history. The surrounding region is rich in Oregon trail history, agriculture, ranching, and timber.

There is a great deal of terrain yet to be developed here. What is available, is a challenging variety of powder and groomed runs, steep faces, mogul and tree skiing. All are carved out of the mountainside that looms 8,000 feet above the valley. There is back-country snow-cat skiing available. For beginners, there is gentle terrain as well. This area is noted for its durable snow pack, which lasts long into spring and, more often than not, the snowfall is powder. Amazingly, there are never lift lines, even though the area has only one chair lift.

As you arrive in the morning, the lodge is filled with the aroma of the fresh baked cinnamon rolls and hamburger buns. Do you ski or eat first?

Reminiscent of the "Slush Cup Races" of Mount Baker in Washington, is the area's annual spring "Snow Rodeo" in which enthusiastic skiers and snowboarders try to gather enough speed to cross a lake of icy, slushy water.

For the cross country skier, there is a nordic trail system beginning at the lodge and circling Anthony Lake, Lily Pad Lake, and the meadows around them.

PHONE NUMBERS:

Information	(503) 963-4599 or
	(503) 856-3277
Snowline	1-800-762-7941

DIRECTIONS:
Anthony Lakes is located between La Grande and Baker City. Driving on I-84, exit at North Powder (Exit 285) and travel west for 19 miles, following signs.

DRIVING TIMES: (estimated)

Seattle	370 miles	6.5 hours
Walla Walla	148 miles	2+ hours
Tri-Cities	160 miles	3 hours
Portland	280 miles	4.5 hours
Pendleton	91 miles	1.5 hours
La Grande	44 miles	1 hour
Baker City	36 miles	45 minutes
Spokane	350 miles	6+ hours
Boise	110 miles	2.5 hours

LIFT PRICES: (1993-94)
Adult $20
Students (10-18) $17
Child (9 and under) $11
Poma only $ 8
Half-day begins at 12:45 pm

DAYS AND HOURS OF OPERATION:
Thursday, Friday   9:00 am to 4:00 pm
Saturday and Sunday   9:00 am to 4:00 pm
CLOSED Monday (except Holiday Mondays) Tuesday and Wednesday
EXCEPTION: Open Thanksgiving Week, Christmas Week and March Spring Vacation Week
CLOSED Christmas Day
Open through April, snow permitting

ANTHONY LAKES INFORMATION AND FACILITIES:

RUNS	16
LIFTS	1 double chair
	1 poma
FOOD	Lodge with cafeteria and deli bar
	(*Fresh* baked bread and rolls)
	"Starbattle Lounge" with live music on
	Saturday, Sun and holidays

AND MORE   Ski Shop - accessories **(503-856-3279)**
Rental/repair - alpine, nordic and
   snowboard
Ski School
RV parking in lot (self-contained)
Sno-park permit

SNOWBOARDING:
Half-pipe
Snowboard rentals

CROSS COUNTRY:
13 km of groomed trails
New trail 1993-94!
Trail pass $7.00

CHILD CARE:
Weekends only   9:30 am to 4:00 pm
Located in the A-frame house next to lodge

SPECIAL INFORMATION:
SNO-PARK PERMIT: Oregon Sno-park permit required for parking lot. Available for purchase in the lodge.
DISABLED LESSONS: Ski school has instructors trained in teaching persons with disabilities.
COLLEGE: Eastern Oregon State college is in La Grande, where there is a good selection of accommodations.
COMMERCIAL TRANSPORTATION: La Grande is served by Amtrak, Greyhound and commercial flights from Portland.
SKIER GROUPS: Groups are welcome and special rates are available. Contact the business office.
PARKING LOT: Upper parking lot can have a large "lake" in it in the spring. Don't drive in unless you have four-wheel drive to get out!
ROAD: Forest Service road driving to ski area contains potholes and frost heaves. Drive carefully.
SKI BUS: Ski bus from La Grande and Baker on weekends, sponsored by the Baker Parks and Recreation Department, call **503-963-6384** for reservations.
LIFT TICKET: Motels in the area offer discount vouchers on your lift ticket - be sure to ask!
SNO-CAT: Sno-cat skiing available, weather permitting.

OVERNIGHT ACCOMMODATIONS:
ANTHONY LAKE   (no accommodations at this time)

BAKER CITY

Eldorado Motel	1-503-523-6494
Super 8	1-503-523-8282
Quality Inn	1-503-523-2242
Best Western Sunridge Inn	1-503-523-6444
Friendship Inn	1-503-523-6571
Royal Motor Inn	1-503-523-6324

NORTH POWDER

Powder River Motel	1-503-898-2829

LA GRANDE

Best Western Pony Soldier Inn	1-503-963-7195
Royal Motor Inn	1-503-963-4154
Stardust Lodge	1-503-963-4166
Greenwell Motel	1-503-963-4134
Super 8	1-503-963-8080
Broken Arrow Lodge	1-503-963-7116

BUSINESS ADDRESS:
Anthony Lakes Mountain Resort
61995 Quail Road
Island City, OR 97850
(503) 856-3277 or
(503) 963-4599 (La Grande office)

Anthony Lakes Spring Rodeo. Captive Photos.

HOODOO AREA

5,703' top elevation   **1,035' vertical drop**

HOODOO SKI AREA

Hoodoo is accessible from both east of the Willamette Valley (Salem, Eugene, etc.) and west of Central Oregon (Sisters and Bend). A family oriented area, it has had skiers on the mountain since 1939.

The area hosts City League and Emerald League racing, a Winter Carnival in February, and on Tuesdays, a "Great Escape" ski day includes ski classes, lunch, and a video review of your skiing day. You can test your racing ability on a complimentary race course (the Perrier Challenge), or join one of the organized ski or snowboard racing programs. Other instruction programs include alpine, nordic, and snowboard.

The mountain runs are well-positioned, with the beginner runs lower on the mountain to the right of the lodge, and the intermediate and advanced runs higher on the slopes. The terrain is less "treed" than many of the Cascade ski areas, promoting a sense of freedom and the ability to do swooping GS turns. Mogul lovers will like Grandstand and Headwall, two ungroomed steeply pitched runs, both under the Green chairlift.

At the base area are two lodges with rental/repair facilities, a ski shop, lockers and food selections which include a memorable home-made soup. Hoodoo also offers "guaranteed skiing," which means that skiers can ski *free* any day from nine to ten a.m. to try out the conditions before purchasing a lift ticket.

Also available is a groomed cross country trail, which begins at the south edge of the parking lot and meanders through seven kilometers of forested terrain.

PHONE NUMBERS:
Information   (503) 342-5540
Snowline   1-800-292-LIFT

DIRECTIONS:
Hoodoo is at the summit of Santiam Pass on Highway 126.
Signs are prominently placed to direct you to turn off the
Highway onto a short road to the ski area. From Eugene take
Highway 126. From Salem take Highway 22. From Bend take
Highway 20. (If you are driving from Eugene, there is a
slightly confusing junction of Highway 20 and Highway 22 as
they join Highway 126. Keep bearing right; remember you are
traveling toward Sisters and Bend.)

DRIVING TIMES: (estimated)

Seattle	305 miles	6 hours
Portland	130 miles	1.5 hours
Bend	36 miles	45 minutes
Salem	88 miles	1.5+ hours
Eugene	86 miles	1.5+ hours

LIFT PRICES: (1993-94)
Adult (9:00 am - 4:00 pm) $20
Adult (all day and night) $4
Child (6 to 12 years) $14
Children under 6 and adults over 65 ski *free*
Half-day begins at 1:00 pm
Night skiing begins at 4:00 pm

DAYS AND HOURS OF OPERATION:
Monday, Tuesday, Thursday, Friday, Saturday, Sunday
9:00 am to 4:00 pm
CLOSED most Wednesdays (some exceptions, call)
Night Skiing Thursday, Friday and Saturday
4:00 pm to 10:00 pm
(In March, only Friday and Saturday nights)

HOODOO INFORMATION AND FACILITIES:

RUNS	17
LIFTS	1 triple chair
	2 double chairs
	1 rope tow
FOOD	2 Day lodges with cafeteria, lounge
	and Pizza Pub

AND MORE   Rental/repair- alpine, nordic and
           snowboard
           Ski School - **(503) 822-3799** ext 16
           Ski Shop - accessories
           RV parking in lot (10 hook-ups)
           Sno -Park permit required
           Complimentary ski check service

SNOWBOARDING:
No half-pipe
Snowboard rentals and lessons

CROSS COUNTRY:
15.8 km of groomed track
(8 new kilometers added in 1993)
Trail pass:
Adults $5.00
Children $4.00
Purchase passes in main lodge office.

SPECIAL INFORMATION:
RACE COURSE: Complimentary race course with NASTAR
format is open on the weekends.
LIFT TICKET: You can "try out" the skiing conditions every day
from 9 to 10 am for *free*. (Hoodoo's way of guaranteeing happy
skiers.)
SNO-PARK PERMIT: Sno-park permits are required in
Hoodoo's parking lots.
NEW SERVICES: 1993-94 season brings a newly remodeled food
service area and menu.
RESORT: Development of the ski area and surrounding
recreational areas is underway for a future destination resort.

OVERNIGHT ACCOMMODATIONS:
BLUE LAKE (11 minutes)
Blue Lake Resort   1-503-595-6671

CAMP SHERMAN (20 minutes)
Metolius River Lodges   1-503-595-6290
Metolius River Resort   1-503-595-6281

BLACK BUTTE
Black Butte Ranch   1-800-452-7455

SISTERS
Best Western Ponderosa   1-503-549-1234
Sisters Motor Lodge   1-503-549-2551

BEND
(see Mount Bachelor accommodations, page 146)

EUGENE
(see Willamette Pass accommodations, page 167)

BUSINESS ADDRESS:
Hoodoo Ski Area
PO Box 20
Highway 20
Sisters, OR 97759
(503) 822-3799

Courtesy of Hoodoo Ski Area.

MOUNT ASHLAND AREA

7,500' top elevation   **1,150' vertical drop**

MOUNT ASHLAND

Families, college students, and skiers from southern Oregon and northern California can be found on the slopes of Mount Ashland. One thing they all share is a smile on their faces that says "great skiing and no lift lines."

As you approach the area, you can get a great view of the mountain, enabling you to start mentally planning which of the 23 runs you are going to ski. The lodge perches to the left of the ski area and necessitates a chairlift ride and some advance planning for your return, but once you are familiar with the layout of the mountain, it ceases to be a concern.

All the runs flow gracefully and naturally from the summit. The longest run is one mile of wide open terrain. There are bowls, moguls, steeps and chutes. About 50% of the terrain is rated for advanced skiers. There is also a good selection of wide open beginner and intermediate terrain and four chair lifts to position you to your favorite run. The information desk in the lodge posts a list of the groomed runs each day to assist with your run selections.

The uniquely designed lodge offers a ski shop, rental and repair, cafeteria and lounge in a cozy and friendly atmosphere. Snowboarders, cross country (Bull Gap trail is accessible from the lodge), and alpine skiers gather to eat and discuss their best experiences of the day.

Mount Ashland is convenient to the city of Ashland, which is famous for its Oregon Shakespearean festival. The plays run from February through October each year. Five other theaters with varied playbills offer even more of a selection of after-ski entertainment, as well as restaurants, stores, and walking tours of this fascinating town of many architectural styles. A visit here can include outdoor, historical, cultural, and exceptional culinary experiences.

PHONE NUMBERS:

Information   (503) 482-2897
Snowline   (503) 482-2754

DIRECTIONS:

Mt Ashland is 18 miles southwest of Ashland. From I-5 taking Exit 6, follow the signs on the two-lane road leading to the ski area. I-5 has a steep grade from Ashland to the turn off (nine miles), then it is another steep climb (nine more miles) to Mount Ashland.

DRIVING TIMES: (estimated)

Seattle	486 miles	8+ hours
Portland	310 miles	5+ hours
Bend	216 miles	4+ hours
Ashland	18 miles	30 minutes
Medford	25 miles	45 minutes

LIFT PRICES: (1993-94)

Adult (weekends and holidays) $24
Adult (weekdays) $16
Child (7 - 12) all days $16
Senior (65+) all days $16
Children 6 and under ski *free*
Half- day begins at 12:30

DAYS AND HOURS OF OPERATION:

Daily skiing   9:00 am to 4:00 pm
Night skiing (beginning in December) is on Thursdays, Fridays, Saturdays   4:00 pm to 10:00 pm
Weather can affect this schedule, call **(503) 482-2754** for latest conditions.

MT ASHLAND INFORMATION AND FACILITIES:

RUNS	23
LIFTS	2 triple chairs
	2 double chairs
FOOD	Lodge with cafeteria and lounge
AND MORE	Rental/repair-alpine and snowboard
	Ski Shop - accessories
	Recreational racing course
	Ski School
	Lockers and ski corral to check equipment

SNOWBOARDING:
No half-pipe
Snowboard rentals

SPECIAL INFORMATION:
ROAD: Obey the posted speed limits on the two-lane road to Mt Ashland.
BUS SERVICE: Scheduled bus service from Medford and Ashland for day or night skiing. **(503) 482-2897**
AIRLINES: Medford-Jackson airport at Medford (11 miles from Ashland) is a commercial airport.
SHAKESPEAREAN FESTIVAL: Ashland is famous for its Shakespearean festival, which begins in February. You can combine skiing during the day and a great repertory performance in the evening! Call **1-800-547-8052** for information and schedules.
NEW SERVICES: 1993-94 season will have widened runs, an enlarged deck, remodeled cafeteria, new rental equipment and a new snow-cat grooming machine.
SNO-PARK PERMIT: Oregon Sno-park permit required for parking lot. Purchase in lodge.

OVERNIGHT ACCOMMODATIONS:
ASHLAND

Ashland Motel	1-503-482-2561
Ashland Knight's Inn	1-503-482-5111
Ashland Valley Inn	1-503-482-2641
Best Western Heritage Inn	1-503-482-6932
Windmill's Ashland Hills Inn	1-800-547-4747
Cedarwood Inn	1-800-547-4141
Mark Antony Hotel	1-800-9-ANTONY
Stratford Inn	1-800-547-4741
Timbers Motel	1-503-482-4242

(More accommodations are available-check with a travel agent)

BUSINESS ADDRESS:
Ski Ashland, Inc.
PO Box 220
Ashland, OR 97520
(503) 482-2897

MOUNT BACHELOR AREA

9,065' top elevation   **3,100' vertical drop**

MOUNT BACHELOR

Mount Bachelor continues to evolve into a better and better area since it first opened in 1958. Emphasis has been on creating skier services and developing a skiable mountain for all abilities. Recent additions include: (1) a mid-mountain lodge (1989) offering a full restaurant and beautiful views of Mount Bachelor and the surrounding Deschutes National forest, (2) a computerized sports facility where skiers can quickly and efficiently go through the process of ski rentals, or shop for their skier needs or souvenirs, and (3) more high speed detachable quad chairlifts. In 1993-94 three new chairlifts were added to the area. All the additions are part of an aggressive ten-year plan, begun in 1985, to create a destination ski resort.

Parents and children will find the day care facilities and children's ski programs exceptional. Child care facilities are offered at both the West Village and Sunrise lodges. They can accommodate infants as young a six weeks up to 12-year-old children.

Cross country skiers enjoy an extensive area, also located at West Village. The trail system begins at the Cross Country Lodge and extends into the valley below the parking lot and around the west side of the mountain.

The entire ski area is accessible from any of the three lodges and parking lots. Most of the runs are intermediate to advanced intermediate on the lower portions of the mountain. All are corduroy groomed, and seem to naturally follow the gently sloped terrain to the base of the mountain. The more challenging upper slopes are barren of trees-you are skiing on a dormant volcano. They include bowl skiing, some wide-open steeper runs, and a ridge run which follows a downhill race course, as well as back side skiing that the experts say is outstanding. Be sure to carry your trail map to guide you around the mountain.

High-speed quads quickly distribute skiers on the mountain, and the use of an "electronic" ticket also facilitates shorter lift lines.

Although there are no on-mountain accommodations, the town of Bend is only 22 miles of easy driving away and has an extensive selection of places to stay and after ski activities. The Bend area is an all-year recreation and destination area with many activities to satisfy skiers.

PHONE NUMBERS:

Information	**(503) 382-2442**
Snowline	**(503) 382-7888**
Reservation Line	**(800) 829-2442**

(access to all on-mountain services)

DIRECTIONS:

Mt Bachelor is located in central Oregon, 22 miles from Bend on Century Drive. It's a nice, easy drive from downtown. Signs are prominent throughout the city of Bend directing you to the ski area from Highway 97.

DRIVING TIMES: (estimated)

Seattle	356 miles	7 hours
Portland	181 miles	3.5 hours
Yakima	226 miles	4 hours
Bend	22 miles	15 minutes
Eugene	121 miles	2.5+ hours
Salem	131 miles	3 hours

LIFT PRICES: (1993-94)

Adults (13+) $33*
Child (7 to 12) $18*
Student (13-17) $25*
Seniors (65+) $19*
Children under 6 ski *free*
Half-day begins at 12:00 pm
*(Electronic Tickets-ask about single days, multi-days, Ten-day mini passes or points passes if you are skiing multiple days)

DAYS AND HOURS OF OPERATION:

Open daily   9:00 am to 4:00 pm
This area has an extended ski season which lasts through June. Call for Spring Summit Season hours which begin after Easter Sunday. **(800-829-2442)**
(Lower lift prices go into effect at this time).
No night skiing.

MT BACHELOR INFORMATION AND FACILITIES:

RUNS	60
LIFTS	4 triple chairlifts
	3 express quads
	3 *new chairlifts* 1993-94
	1 detachable triple
	1 double chair
	2 rope tows
FOOD	Six day lodges: Sunrise, Blue, West Village, Pine Marten (mid-mountain), Eagan and the Cross Country Center
	Pine Marten Lodge - buffet, deli, entrees, and gourmet restaurant, South Sister (reservations 1-800-829-2442)
	Sunrise Lodge - deli, cafeteria and bar
	Blue Lodge- cafeteria with American and Italian dishes
	West Village Lodge - deli, bakery, broiler, pizzeria, cafeteria, lounge and sports bar
	Eagan Lodge - no food service
	Cross Country Lodge - lunch service
AND MORE	Rental/repair - alpine and snowboard available at Bachelor Ski and Sports, Blue and Sunrise Lodges
	Rental/repair - cross country at Cross Country Center
	Ski Shop - equipment and accessories at Bachelor Ski and Sports, smaller shops in Blue, Sunrise, Pine Marten, and Cross Country Lodges
	Ski Corral- day, overnight and baskets
	NASTAR - Wednesday through Saturday
	REC RACING- Marborough Ski Challenge (coin-operated race course) 50¢
	RV parking - self contained and attended in designated area only
	Ski School - Skier development centers at West Village Base, Sunrise Lodge and Pine Marten Lodge

SNOWBOARDING:

No half-pipe
Snowboard lessons and rentals

CHILD CARE:
West Village and Sunrise Lodges
Operates seven days a week 8:30 am to 4:30 pm
Ages 6 weeks to 12 years (West Village Lodge)
Ages 6 weeks to 7 years (Sunrise Lodge)
State licensed
Reservations recommended
1-800-829-2442 or
(509) 382-2442 or **(509) 382-2607**
Lunches may be purchased or brought.
Escort service to ski school classes provided.

CROSS COUNTRY:
Cross Country Center Lodge in West Village
Rental/repair
50 km of trails
Adult $9

SPECIAL INFORMATION:
RESORT: Mt Bachelor is a full service resort with nearby amenities that make it a year-round destination resort with an extended ski season through June.
AIRPORT: Redmond has a commercial airport with limo service and rentals, and Bend is served by Amtrak (to Chemult) and bus lines.
AREA BUS: *Free* shuttle service between lodges on half-hour.
BEND BUS: *Free* daily shuttle from Bend Corporate offices (335 SW Century Drive) to mountain.
Weekdays: Up to Mt Bachelor-8:15 am, 9:30 am, 11:15 am
            Down to Bend-10:30 am, 2:00 pm, 3:20 and 4:30 pm
Weekends: same schedule, but add a 7:00 am bus
ATM: ATM machine at West Village.
SKI SCHOOL DISABLED PROGRAM: Ski school has a "Bold Program" instruction for visually impaired skiers.
ROAD: The road between Sisters and Bend is being widened and improved in 1993.

OVERNIGHT ACCOMMODATIONS:
CENTRAL RESERVATIONS   1-800-800-8334

RESORTS
Sunriver Lodge   1-503-593-1221
Inn of the Seventh Mountain   1-503-382-8711
Mt Bachelor Village   1-503-389-5900
Riverhouse   1-503-389-3111
Eagle Crest   1-800-845-8491

BEND
Best Western Entrada   1-503-382-4080
Thunderbird Motel   1-503-382-7011
Red Lion Motel   1-503-382-8384
Holiday Motel   1-503-382-4620
Dunes Motel   1-503-382-6811
Westward Ho!   1-503-382-2111
Touch of Class   1-503-389-9600
Motel West   1-503-389-5577
(more available through central reservations)

BUSINESS ADDRESS:
Mount Bachelor, Inc.
PO Box 1031
Bend, OR 97709-1031
(503) 382-2442

MOUNT HOOD MEADOWS AREA

7,300' top elevation   2,777' vertical drop

MOUNT HOOD MEADOWS

Mount Hood Meadows, nearly 2,00 skiable acres, contains every kind of skiable terrain. This area has developed gradually over the last 25 years. There are gentle sloping beginner runs and steep canyons for experts. There are cleared, packed trails, bumps and bowls, race training areas, and wide open cruising runs. And, exclusively for snowboarders, there is a run and half-pipe area. A new high-speed detachable quad chairlift will be completed for the 1993-94 ski season, which will help transport the many skiers who flock here for fun skiing and lessons.

The largest of the Mt Hood ski areas, Meadows offers an extensive "buffet" of ski lesson options, and plays host to many fund-raising events and race series. Alpine lessons for all abilities are scheduled weekdays and weekends for ages four and up. Snowboarding instructors are available to introduce you to the sport or assist in developing your skills on the area's varied terrain and conditions. The Mt Hood Meadow's ski school is the largest ski school in Oregon, and has programs which include instruction for cross country and physically disabled skiers as well.

The large base lodge accommodates huge numbers of weekend skiers as do the large parking lots, which have shuttle service to the lodge. Dining can include everything from a slice of pizza to a buffet of rotisserie chicken, and also a salad bar. There's a buffaloburger on the menu, in addition to the regular hamburgers, fries, and soft drinks.

Meadows has a proposed plan for a twenty-year expansion. Once completed, it will place Mt Hood Meadows among the year-round destination resorts of the Pacific Northwest.

PHONE NUMBERS:

Information	(503) 337-2222 ext 210
Information - Portland	(503) 246-SKIS
Snowline	(503) 227- SNOW
Ski School	(503) 337-2222 ext 288

DIRECTIONS:

Mt Hood Meadows is located on the eastern slope of Mt Hood off Highway 35. The turn-off is well marked.
From I-5 north of Vancouver, exit onto I-206; after crossing the Columbia River, exit onto I-84 to Hood River. At Hood River go south on Highway 35. (Or, exit at Gresham onto Highway 26, which takes you southeast around Mt Hood and is also the route to Timberline and Skibowl.)
From I-5 south of Portland, exit onto I-206 and again exit at Gresham onto Highway 26 or I-84.
You can also reach this area from central Oregon (Bend) via Highway 97, then Highway 26 at Madras.

DRIVING TIMES: (estimated)

Hood River	30 miles	40 minutes
Seattle	235 miles	5 hours
Portland (Highway 26)	73 miles	1.5 hours
Portland (I-84)	85 miles	1.5 hours
(less traffic on 1-84 which connects to Hood River)		
Spokane	364 miles	6.5 hours
Govnmt Camp	12 miles	15 minutes
Bend	106 miles	2+ hours

LIFT PRICES: (1993-94)

Adult $27
Junior (7 to 12) $17
Seniors (65+) $17
Children 6 and under $6
Half-day begins at 12:00 pm
Night skiing begins at 4:00 pm

DAYS AND HOURS OF OPERATION:

Open daily

Monday and Tuesday	9:00 am to 4:00 pm
Wednesday to Saturday	9:00 am to 10:00 pm
Sunday	9:00 am to 7:00 pm

MT HOOD MEADOWS INFORMATION AND FACILITIES:

RUNS	25
LIFTS	7 double chairs
	1 quad
	1 triple chair
	1 rope tow
FOOD	2 side by side lodges
	North Lodge and South Lodge
	North Lodge has espresso and potato bar, bar and grill, and convenience food.
	South Lodge has sports lounge, deli, buffet, pizzeria and beerstube.
AND MORE	Rental/repair - alpine-snowboard
	Ski shop - accessories
	Ski School -**(503) 246-1348** ext. 288
	NASTAR
	Coin-op race course
	Ski and basket check
	RV parking (with Sno-Park permit) in lot (self contained)

SNOWBOARDING:

Half-pipe and snowboarding area
Snowboard rentals and lessons
Special racing and competitive events are held here.
Call for schedule.

CROSS COUNTRY:

26 km of trails
Track fee: $7.00
Separate area from alpine area, follow signs to the right as you drive to ski area from the main highway
Rentals in lodge
NO food service

SPECIAL INFORMATION:

SKI SCHOOL: Ski School offers a wide variety of programs and packages which includes instruction for the physically disabled. **(503) 246-1348**
READERBOARD: On Highway 26 at Sandy there is an informational sign at the Safeway store, which gives updated traffic and road conditions.

SNO-PARK PERMIT: Sno-Park permit is required. Purchase seasonal or daily parking permit in lodge.

ATM: ATM machine is located in the walkway between the lodges.

BUS/LIFT: This is a service offered which provides round- trip transportation from Portland and a lift ticket on weekends and school holidays from Christmas through March. It has five stops on the way, call **503-287-5438** for information.

CHILD CARE: There is *no child care* offered at this area, but there are a great variety of ski school programs designed for children four and older.

ANNIVERSARY: Mt Hood Meadows celebrated its 25th season in 1992-93.

NEW LIFTS: Look for a new high-speed detachable quad chairlift in the 1993-94 season.

MEDICAL CENTER: There is a seven-day-a-week medical center on site which provides emergency first aid and medical services on the mountain, to skiers as well as to visitors, motorists, hikers and area residents.

OVERNIGHT ACCOMMODATIONS:

The accommodations listed below are also used for the Cooper Spur, Timberline, and Skibowl ski areas as well. The three areas are all within ten miles of each other--a skier's dream come true!

COOPER SPUR
Inn at Cooper Spur   1-503-352-6692

HOOD RIVER
Hood River Inn (Best Western)	1-503-386-2200
Meredith Gorge Motel	1-503-386-1515
Hood River Motel	1-503-386-1900
Love's Riverview Lodge	1-503-386-8719
Prater's Motel	1-503-386-3566
Vagabond Lodge	1-503-386-2292

TIMBERLINE
Timberline Lodge   1-503-272-3311
(A National Historic Landmark)

GOVERNMENT CAMP
England's Lodging	1-503-272-3350
Falcon's Crest Inn	1-503-272-3403
Huckleberry Inn	1-503-272-3325

Mt Hood Inn	1-800-443-7777
Summit Meadow Cabins	1-503-272-3494
Thunderhead Lodge Condominiums	1-503-272-3368

WELCHES

Mt Hood RV Village	1-503-622-4011
The Resort at the Mountain	1-503-622-3101
Whispering Woods Condominiums	1-503-622-3171

SANDY

| Shamrock Deluxe Motel | 1-503-622-4911 |

BUSINESS ADDRESS:

Mt Hood Meadows
6420 S W Macadam Ave
Suite 216
Portland, OR 97201
(503) 246-1348 or (503) 246-1810

SKIBOWL AREA

5,066', 5,026', 4,656' top elevations   1,500' vertical drop

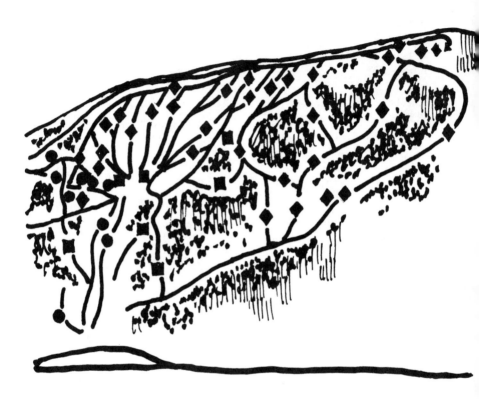

SKIBOWL

Whatever the season, Skibowl has an activity to interest you. In addition to winter skiing, snowboarding and sleigh rides, in the summer this area offers horseback rides, hay rides, catered events under a tent or in the lodge, mountain biking and their very unusual alpine slide . The entire mountain and slide can be rented by groups, businesses or families.

Snowboarders have their very own center here, located at the Multopor Lodge (referred to as Skibowl East). There are rentals, lessons, special lift prices and a newly constructed half-pipe (1993) which meets the Snowboarders Association standards.

There are actually two areas here which are connected by the Sleigh Ride trail. The Multopor Mountain base and area is to the left, and has its own parking and lodge. The Skibowl Peak/Tom Dick Peak area has its base area, lodge and parking on a turn-out from the main highway. Combined, the areas have 65 runs, trails and bowls to challenge and interest every level of skier. The grooming is to corduroy perfection and allows you to cruise some exciting runs like Reynolds Run, which is an Olympic giant slalom course.

If racing interests you, there is a NASTAR and an automated race course in addition to many racing programs for ages six and up. The area is host to a variety of skiing and snowboard competitions from extreme snowboarding , to Junior Olympic qualifying races, and speed skiing championships.

On the weekends, if you like to explore out-back areas, there are *free* guided tours by the ski patrol. At night, almost half of the area is under lights, which allows the area to advertise that it is the largest single night ski area in America.

PHONE NUMBERS:
Information   (503) 222-4158
Snowline   (503) 222-BOWL

DIRECTIONS:
Skibowl (formerly Multopor and Mirror Mountain) is on
Highway 26 near Mt Hood, just prior to Government Camp.
Going east or west, the exit is clearly marked. The exit to
Skibowl East (the Multopor side) is through the business
district of Government Camp, then across Highway 26 via
a bridge.

DRIVING TIMES: (estimated)
See Mt Hood Meadows and add or subtract 15 minutes.
This area is 52 miles from Portland, and a little over an hour's
drive in good weather. There is a readerboard at the Sandy
Safeway which posts road conditions and weather in the
Mt Hood area.

LIFT PRICES: (1993-94)
Adult $22 day skiing
        $12 night skiing
Junior (11 and under)
        $15 day skiing
        $10 night skiing
Night skiing begins at 4:30 pm
Half-day begins at 11:00 am

DAYS AND HOURS OF OPERATION:
Skibowl's operating hours may vary from those listed below.
Call **(503) 222-BOWL** for current hours.

Winter
Monday to Thursday 9:00 am to 10:00 pm
Friday   9:00 am to 11:00 pm
Saturday   8:30 am to 11:00 pm
Sunday   8:30 am to 10:00 pm

Spring
Spring schedule changes about mid March - call information.

SKI BOWL INFORMATION AND FACILITIES:
RUNS   65
                (33 lighted night runs)

LIFTS	4 double chairs
	5 rope tows
FOOD	East Lodge - cafeteria and lounge
	West Lodge - cafeteria and beerstube
	Warming hut on mountain - cafeteria
AND MORE	Rental/repair - alpine (at Skibowl West)
	Rental/repair - snowboard (at Skibowl East)
	Ski School
	Ski Shop - accessories
	NASTAR
	Coin-op race course 50¢
	Ski check
	RV parking in lot - self-contained and
	with a Sno-Park permit

SNOWBOARDING:

Half-pipe and snowboarding area
Snowboard Center at Skibowl East
Rentals and lessons

SPECIAL INFORMATION:

TOURS: Guided Ski Patrol tours of the out-back bowls on Saturday and Sunday at 11:00 am and 2:00 pm.
GROUPS: Groups can rent the mountain and/or lodges, call **503-222-4158.**
CATERING: Catering is available for meetings and events.
RACING: For information, call **503-222-BOWL.**
SLEIGH RIDES: Sleigh rides available, call **503-222-2695.**
SUMMER: During the summer, Skibowl has a half-mile long alpine slide, mountain biking, can-am race carts, and guided horseback riding.

OVERNIGHT ACCOMMODATIONS:

See Mount Hood Meadows for listings, page 152.

BUSINESS ADDRESS:

Mt Hood Skibowl
Winter and Summer Resort
PO Box 280
Ski Bowl, OR 97028
(503) 222-2695

TIMBERLINE AREA

7,000' top elevation (winter)   1,500' vertical drop
8,500' top elevation (summer)   1,500' vertical drop

TIMBERLINE

Many things combine to make this ski area a most unique skiing experience. Timberline Lodge, part of the National Park system, rests majestically above this ski area parking lot, welcoming all arriving travelers. This dramatic and picturesque lodge is a popular destination for many travelers summer and winter.

The ski area day lodge, Wy'east, is in sharp architectural contrast to this historically designed and hand-made lodge from the 1930's. Built in 1980, it nestles into the hillside and holds a treasure of commissioned artworks, furnishings and services. The lodge is massive, but comfortable, and functionally designed to accommodate all skier needs, from ticketing, ski rental and repairs, ski school offices, and cafeteria, to souvenir and ski accessory shopping.

Wy'east lodge sits above most of the ski area. This is unique in that you ski down from the lodge during the winter skiing months. There's a special area just for beginners on a gently-sloped hill with a slow chairlift to help you build confidence. For intermediate to advanced skiers, there are numerous tree lined runs carved into the slopes. You can also take a quick ride up above the treeline on the Magic Mile quad chairlift, which places you on a snowfield, then you can design your own combinations of runs on the way down.

Snowboarders have their own "Bone Zone" area (no skiing here) in addition to two half-pipes. They can also choose to test their skills by participating in snowboard competitions sponsored by Burton or City League racing held here during the winter season.

Telemark skiers can learn the techniques of cross country or downhill skiing. Children can learn the basics in the Skiwee clinics. Basic to advanced ski and snowboarding lessons are available here as well. If you like racing, there is a coin-operated ski racing run to challenge your downhill skills.

Timberline has an extended skiing season, which also makes this area fairly unique in the Pacific Northwest. As the deep snows of winter melt away, the Palmer lift, which goes *up* the mountain onto the snowfield/glacier area, begins its operation, (usually in early June). Outside summer temperatures on Mt Hood can vary from below freezing to 90 degrees.

PHONE NUMBERS:

Information   (503) 272-3311
Portland Area   (503) 231-7979
Snowline   (503) 222-2211
Ski School   (503) 231-5402

DIRECTIONS:

Timberline is located on the South slope of Mt Hood- off
Highway 26 just past Government Camp about 3 miles off the
main highway. The road from Highway 26 is steep and
winding, but well-maintained. There are good directional signs
to guide you.

LIFT PRICES:

Adult   (13 and older)
          Day and night skiing $28
          Day only $26
Child   (12 and under)
          Day and night skiing $17
          Day only $15
Children 6 and under ski *free* with a parent.
Monday and Tuesday Special, all ages $16
Half-day options:
          9:00 am to 1:00 pm or
          1:00 pm to 10:00 pm or 4:00 pm to 10:00 pm
Night skiing begins at 4:00 pm

DAYS AND HOURS OF OPERATION:

Winter
Sunday, Monday Tuesday 9:00 am to 5:00 pm
Wednesday through Saturday 9:00 am to 10:00 pm
Afternoon hours are changed in Spring around April 1st

Spring
Daily 8:00 am to 2:30 pm
Spring hours change to Summer on June 12th

Summer
Daily 7:00 am to 1:30 pm (Quad and Palmer Lift)

TIMBERLINE INFORMATION AND FACILITIES:

RUNS	31
LIFTS	3 double chairs
	1 triple chair
	1 high speed express quad
	1 double chair (Palmer Lift operating summer only with express quad)
FOOD	Wy'East Day Lodge-cafeteria and lounge
	Timberline Lodge-restaurant and deli
AND MORE	Ski and gift shop - accessories and apparel
	Ski School-alpine, snowboard and telemark
	Rental/repair - alpine, snowboard
	Ski-keep
	Coin-op racing
	RV parking in lot -(self contained only)
	Sno-Park permits required

SNOWBOARDING:

Two half-pipes and a "Bone Zone" (special area for snowboarders only)
Snowboard rentals and lessons

SPECIAL INFORMATION:

NATIONAL LANDMARK: Timberline Lodge is a National Historic Landmark built in 1937. Don't leave the area without visiting this remarkable building to appreciate the craftsmanship, as well as learn its history.

EVENTS: Many alpine and snowboard competitions and fund-raising events take place here. Call to inquire.

BUS: Bus transportation and lift ticket packages are available from the Portland area from about mid- December to the end of March. Call **(503) 231-7979** for information and reservations.

ATM: ATM machine in Wy'east Day lodge near the store.

RESTAURANT: Fine dining is available in the Cascade Room of the Timberline Lodge.

OVERNIGHT ACCOMMODATIONS:

See Mt Hood Meadows for more accommodations, page 152.
The closest accommodation is at Timberline Lodge, which
shares the parking lot and offers ski packages.

TIMBERLINE LODGE

Room Reservations	1-800-547-1406
from Portland	1-503-231-5400

BUSINESS ADDRESS:

Timberline Ski Area
Timberline Lodge, OR 97028
(503) 321-7979

Mt Hood Recreation Association
P O Box 342
Welches, OR 97067
(503) 622-3017

Courtesy of Timberline Lodge.

WILLAMETTE PASS AREA

6,666' top elevation   **1,525' vertical drop**

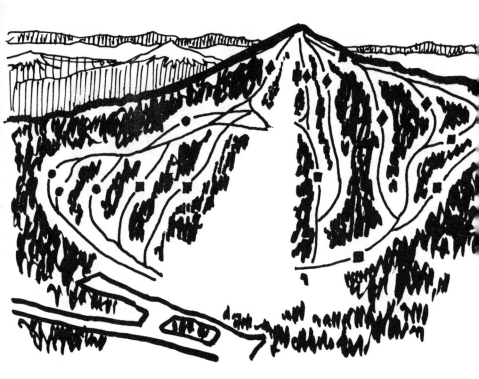

WILLAMETTE PASS

A scenic drive from the west or east, Willamette Pass attracts families and individuals who find its long, wide, gently sloped tree-lined runs the perfect setting to develop and test their giant slalom skills. Yet it also offers some intense and challenging runs for expert skiers.

Just to the right of the lodge is a beginner area and slow moving chair lift to help new skiers gain confidence. On the rest of the mountain (there are two sides to it), there are 28 more trails which enable you to advance and test your abilities. All are long and uninterrupted by cross overs or cat trails. These are great cruising runs which offer you the choice of beginner, intermediate and advanced skiing terrain. The advanced runs are steeper in pitch and include moguls carved out of the 300 inches of snowpack. Top to bottom, the longest run is just over two miles!

If you want to watch speed skiers compete or train, this is the place to come. The USSA Speed Skiing team races and trains here, and recreational speed skiing clinics are offered for those who seek to experience this thrill as well. Ski school programs are offered for alpine, nordic, telemark, snowboard and racing. Eagle Peak contains the perfect terrain for all these sports.

Skier services are all within the massive lodge at the base of the mountain. There are spectacular views of the mountain from the lodge or the deck.

The ticketing is an unusual feature of this ski area, where options for your best skiing value are a major consideration. You can ski by the hour, by the vertical foot, or by the day. You can purchase a five-day mini pass, a Club Vertical pass, a corporate-account pass, or a regular season pass. All are electronically controlled by a SKI KEY pass (a wrist bracelet ticket), which is purchased and updated yearly thereafter.

Cross country skiers have access to 20 kilometers of groomed and tracked trails. There is a nordic center at the west end of the main parking lot.

Snowboarders also have their own area (and the entire mountain as well) which is complete with a half-pipe. Lessons are available, and if you rent a snowboard package, you can receive a complimentary group lesson.

PHONE NUMBERS:

Information	(503) 484-5030
Snowline	(503) 345-SNOW

DIRECTIONS:

Willamette Pass is about 70 miles Southeast of Eugene off I-5 to Highway 58.

Exit I-5 on 188A to Goshen. You will not enter the town, but will continue east on the two lane scenic Highway 58 to the ski area.

DRIVING TIMES: (estimated)

Crescent Junction	7 miles	12 minutes
Oakridge	27 miles	30 minutes
Eugene	70 miles	1.5+ hours
Portland	180 miles	3.5 hours
Bend	86 miles	2 hours

LIFT PRICES: (1993-94)

Adult	$22*
Youth (6 to 12)	$16*
Child 5 and under	$1*
Senior (65+)	$11*

Half -day skiing begins at 12:30 pm
Night skiing begins at 4:00 pm

*There is an additional fee of $2.00 to purchase a SKI KEY, which gives you access to the lifts. It is reusable throughout the season, and can be updated the following year for a $1.00 charge. The SKI KEY is a wrist (velcro-strap) bracelet, which has two raised bumps that are lined up with dots on a meter device at each lift. (It takes a little dexterity to line the dots up, but gets easier with practice!)

There are several options in purchasing lift passes - consider them for your best value.

DAYS AND HOURS OF OPERATION:

Daily skiing	Wednesday to Sunday	9:00 am to 4:00 pm
Night skiing	Friday and Saturday	4:00 pm to 9:00 pm
CLOSED	Monday and Tuesday	

WILLAMETTE PASS INFORMATION AND FACILITIES:

RUNS 29

LIFTS 4 triple chairs
1 double chair
1 rope tow

FOOD Cascade Summit Lodge-restaurant and lounge

AND MORE Ski shop- accessories and apparel
Ski School- race programs
Rental/repair-alpine and snowboard
Snowmaking
RV parking in upper lot with Sno-park permit and validated overnight parking permit, self-contained only and limited space available, call for reservations **(503) 484-5030**

SNOWBOARDING:

Two half-pipes
Snowboard rentals and lessons

CROSS COUNTRY:

20 km of trails (new in 1990-91)
Nordic Center in west end of parking lot
Open Wednesday to Sunday 8:30 am to 4:30 pm
Trail Pass:
Adult $6
Youth $4
Rental/repair

CHILD CARE: (in Ski Patrol Building by Lodge)

State certified
Ages 15 months to 10 years
One-day advance reservations **(503) 484-5030** are required to take advantage of the complimentary care for children accompanied by a skiing/ticketed parent. Otherwise, there is a fee charged, and it is by space available.
OPEN: 8:30 am to 4:30 pm (lunch *not* included)
CLOSED: during lunch from noon to one. Children must be picked up prior to noon.

SPECIAL INFORMATION:

SPEED SKIING: Willamette Pass is the primary training center for the US Speed Skiing team.

EVENTS: It is also host to many USSA races, Nordic events and Snowboard competitions. Check the season's schedule in case an event interests you.

TRANSPORTATION: Eugene has a commercial airport and is served by bus and train.

COLLEGE: The University of Oregon is in Eugene. There are usually plenty of accommodations, but if a University event is taking place it can limit the lodging facilities available.

SUNRIVER: Sunriver Resort (towards Bend) is another option for vacation planning.

OBSTACLE SIGN: There is a sign used on the mountain that warns of obstacles. A triangle with red border and an exclamation mark inside means *watch out* when you see it.

OVERNIGHT ACCOMMODATIONS:

WILLAMETTE PASS

Willamette Pass Inn (7 miles east)	1-503-433-2211

ODELL LAKE

Odell Lake Lodge (6 miles east)	1-503-433-2540
Shelter Cove Resort	1-503-433-2548

OAKRIDGE

Oakridge Best Western	1-800-782-2212
Cascade Motel	1-503-782-2602
Ridgeview Motel	1-503-782-3430
Failor's Motel	1-503-433-2710

EUGENE

Campus Inn	1-503-343-3374
Barron's Motor Inn	1-503-342-6383
Best Western Greentree	1-503-485-2727
Eugene Travelodge	1-503-342-1109
Valley River Inn	1-503-687-0123

(These are just a few of a large selection)

SUNRIVER

Sunriver Resort (45 miles)	1-800-962-1770

BUSINESS ADDRESS:

Willamette Pass Ski Corporation
PO Box 5509
Eugene, OR 97405
(503) 484-5030

ADDITIONAL OREGON SKI AREAS

These areas are smaller and operate on a varying schedule (usually only open on weekends or limited weekdays). They are sometimes run by organizations or groups local to the area. They lack the size and amenities of destination resorts, but can still provide a unique skiing experience. These areas are particularly enjoyable with young skiers or for families seeking a fun day of skiing without paying large lift fees. Each is definitely worth checking out. The phone numbers can change depending on the organization or person responsible for managing the area each year. In some cases, I have just listed the area code instead of a phone listing. Call information for a current listing.

COOPER SPUR (near Hood River and Mt Hood Ski Areas)
(503) 352-7803
1 T-bar
1 rope tow
5 runs
Rental/repair
Day lodge with cafeteria and snack bar
Cooper Spur Inn (log cabins) and restaurant
(503) 352-6037

DIXIE SKI BOWL (near Prairie City , Highway 26)
(503)
1 rope tow

SPOUT SPRINGS (neat Weston, Highway 204)
(503) 556-2015
2 chair lifts
1 rope tow
2 T-bars
Ski School
2 cafeterias
Ski Shop
Rental/repair

SUMMIT SKI AREA (near Government Camp, Mt Hood)
(503) 272-0256
1 double chair
1 rope tow
Ski School
Day lodge with cafeteria
Ski store
Cross Country trails and rentals

WARNER CANYON (near Lakeview, Highway 140)
(503) 947-2932
1 T-bar
Day lodge with cafeteria

Mount Ashland, lodge and mountain.

DIRECTORY OF SKI ORGANIZATIONS

ADAPTIVE SKIING
(for people with disabilities)

THE SKIFORALL FOUNDATION
Bellefield Office Park, Arbor Building
1621-114th AVE SE, Suite 132
Bellevue, WA 98004-6905
(206) 462-0978
TDD **(206) 462-0979**

This organization provides instruction in alpine and nordic
skiing in their winter program. Their summer instruction
program offers a variety of sports. All are designed and taught
to people with all types of disabilities.

SKI AREA ASSOCIATIONS

PACIFIC NORTHWEST SKI AREAS ASSOCIATION
PO Box 2325
Seattle, WA 98111-2325
206-623-3777

An organization whose focus is to develop, coordinate and
monitor programs designed to enhance the well-being of both
the ski industry as a whole and its members individually.

MT HOOD RECREATION ASSOCIATION
PO Box 342
Welches, OR 97067
503-622-4822

Organization formed to promote tourism (mainly skiing) on
Mount Hood.

SKI INSTRUCTORS

PROFESSIONAL SKI INSTRUCTORS OF AMERICA NORTHWEST (PSIA-NW)
11204 Des Moines Memorial Drive
Seattle, WA 98168
206-244-8541

This regional division of PSIA oversees the training, educational requirements and certification for ski instructors in the Northwest.

PROFESSIONAL SKI INSTRUCTORS ASSOCIATION (PSIA)
5541 Central Avenue
Boulder, CO 80301
518-783-1143

This national organization oversees the training, educational requirements and certification for ski instructors. There are nine divisions in the United States.

SKI PATROL

NATIONAL SKI PATROL
133 S Van Gorden St
Suite 100
Lakewood, CO 80228-1700
303-988-1111

This organization oversees the training, certification, and the qualifications, etc., for volunteers and professionals who administer first-aid and patrol the ski areas.

SKI RACING

NASTAR
PO Box 4580
Aspen, CO 81612

National Standard Race courses are race events held at participating ski areas for recreational racers.

UNITED STATES SKI ASSOCIATION (USSA)
P O Box 100
Park City, UT 84060
801-649-9090

This is the national membership arm of the US Skiing organization. It has over 30,000 member athletes, officials, coaches and supporters and it governs the skiing competitions within the United States. (USSA) See regional divisions below.

INTERMOUNTAIN DIVISION
P O Box 58956
Salt Lake City, UT 84158
801-582-5634

This is a geological division of the USSA membership. It includes the southeastern area of Idaho, the eastern corners of Wyoming, and northern Utah, and the northeastern corner of Nevada.

PACIFIC NORTHWEST SKI ASSOCIATION (PNSA)
640 N W Gillman Blvd #104
Issaquah, WA 98027
206-392-4220

This is a geological division of the USSA membership which includes Washington, Oregon and Northern Idaho.

ADDITIONAL SKI ORGANIZATIONS

ANCIENT SKIERS INC
7233 80th Ave SE
Mercer Island, WA 98040
206-232-0388

This is an organization for skiers who are 60-plus and who have skied the Northwest in earlier years. The group continues to "mingle and mangle" together, skiing and re-uniting to share memories of northwest skiing history.

PASS REPORT PHONE NUMBERS:

Also refer to Snowline phone listing for each ski area.

WASHINGTON
1-900-407-7277 (Washington State Department Of
 Transportation)
1-900-940-PASS
1-206-976-7623
1-206-455-7900
1-206-455-7788 (TDD users)
1-509-976-7623 October to March (east side of Cascades)

OREGON
1-509-976-7277 (in Oregon)
1-503-889-3999 (where 976 service is unavailable)

IDAHO
(208) 336-6600 Statewide
(208) 376-8028 Southern Idaho

SKI REPORT PHONE LISTINGS:

CASCADE Ski Report: Seattle **(206) 634-0200**
                        Tacoma **(206) 922-0599**
                        Everett **(206) 353-7440**

WASHINGTON
State Cross Country Hotline: **(206) 632-2021**

MT HOOD Ski Area Report: **(503) 222-9951**

SELECTED REFERENCE BOOKS

Brewster, David and Stephanie Irving
Northwest Best Places
Seattle, WA: Sasquatch Books, 1993.

Burgdorfer, Rainer
Backcountry Skiing in Washington's Cascades
Seattle, WA: The Mountaineers, 1986.

Canniff, Kiki
A Camper's Guide to Oregon and Washington
Portland, OR: Kiki Enterprises, 1992.

Conley, Cort
Idaho For the Curious
Cambridge, ID: Backeddy Books, 1982.

Faubion, William
William Faubion's You are Invited to the Best Choices Off Oregon's Interstates
Portland, Or: Apple Press Publications, 1986.

Featherston, Phyllis and Barbara F Ostler
Bed and Breakfast Guide
Norwalk, CT: National Bed and Breakfast Assn, 1993.

Gillette, Ned
Cross Country Skiing, 3rd Edition
Seattle, WA: The Mountaineers, 1991.

Kirkendall, Tom and Vicky Spring
Cross Country Ski Tours 1
Seattle, WA: The Mountaineers, 1988.

Kirkendall, Tom and Vicky Spring
Cross Country Ski Tours 2
Seattle, WA: The Mountaineers, 1988.

Lanier, Pamela
Bed and Breakfasts, The Complete Guide to Inn and Guesthouses
Oakland, CA: Lanier Publications Intl, LTD, 1992.

Larson, Eric and William Faubion
   William Faubion's You Are Cordially Invited to the Best Choices in Western Washington
   Medford, OR: Cable and Gray, 1987.

Litman, Tom and Suzanne Kort
   Washington Off the Beaten Path
   Old Saybrook, CT: Globe Pequot Press, 1993.

Loftus, Bill
   Idaho Handbook
   Chico, CA: Moon Publications, 1992.

Mainwaring, William
   Exploring the Mt Hood Loop
   Salem, OR: Westridge Press, LTD, 1992.

McFarlane, Marilyn
   Best Places to Stay in the Pacific Northwest
   Boston, MA: Houghton Mifflin Co, 1992.

Montgomery, Miles
   You Are Cordially Invited to the Best Choices of Eastern Washington and Northern Idaho
   Medford, OR: Cable and Gray, 1988.

Riegert, Ray
   Ultimate Washington
   Berkeley, CA: Ulysses Press, 1993.

Vjielbig, Klindt
   Cross-Country Ski Routes of Oregon's Cascades
   Seattle, WA: The Mountaineers, 1984.

Vokac, David
   The Great Towns of the Pacific Northwest
   San Diego, CA: West Press, 1987.

Walter, Claire
   Rocky Mountain Skiing
   Golden, CO: Fulcrum Publishing, 1992.

American Automobile Association
Oregon Washington Tour Book
Heathrow, FL: American Automobile Association
(AAA), 1993.

American Automobile Association
Idaho Montana Wyoming Tour Book
Heathrow, FL: American Automobile Association
(AAA), 1993.

Insight Guides
The Pacific Northwest
Singapore: Apa Publications (HK) LTD
Houghton Mifflin Co., 1993.

INDEX

ABOUT THE AUTHOR

Cookie Crosetto began skiing at the age of six at Leavenworth, Washington. She is a graduate of the University of Washington, is married and has two grown sons. The idea for this book began in 1984, when her sons began ski racing. Their weekend travel to ski competitions throughout the Northwest necessitated having ski area information which would make each area a weekend's destination. Cookie shared her original information with other ski racing parents in a limited edition book, *Finding Your Way and Where to Stay* (1989), which benefited the Alpental-Snoqualmie Ski Foundation. She has served as secretary, president, and fund-raising director of the Alpental-Snoqualmie Ski Foundation; has done volunteer work for the Pacific Northwest Ski Association; and has served on committees to develop the Debbie Armstrong High School Ski racing program, the Evergreen race series, and the Washington Centennial Games. She continues to be an avid recreational skier and Northwest ski area traveler.

Author researching at Anthony Lakes.